One at a Time

THE LIFE OF ROMA LEE COURVISIER

Bonnie Newell

Bonnie Newell

3-1-14

Joel & Jen,

I encourage you to seek God's will for your lives and live in it every day.

You are loved more than words can express

Jeremiah 29:11-13

Love,

Mom

On the cover: Roma Lee and the Little Grandma at Caja de Agua.

ISBN-13: 13-978-0615971049

Printed in the United States of America.

Dedication

This book is dedicated:

- to my husband, Eric, who has always been a model of faith, evidenced by his passion for sharing the gospel with the lost and his love of people.
- to my uncle, Dean Flora. As a child, I knew that when he came to visit while on furlough, I would hear exciting stories of God's work in Panama. His courage for the Lord has left an everlasting impression on my life. As a sixteen-year-old in 1965, it was in Panama that I first witnessed people living in cardboard houses in extreme poverty. My life has never been the same.
- to my parents, Everett and Lura Callison, who consistently lived a life of total commitment to the Lord. I learned from them that living out the love of Christ is a lifestyle.
- to the next generation of missionaries, both at home and abroad. There is no place more important than to be in the center of God's will. I encourage each one to find it and live there.

Table of Contents

Acknowledgements

I would like to acknowledge the Middletown Area Christian Writers for their constructive criticism of this manuscript over the eighteen months it has been in process. All members are writers in their own right and have provided valuable insight, not only into the mechanics of writing, but into the importance of always being in touch with the inspiration of the Holy Spirit in every written endeavor.

I would like to acknowledge Roma Lee for permitting the use of newsletters from her personal files for inclusion in the book.

Preface

In the spring of 2012, on a Sunday night after teaching an elective class at our church, my husband and I were in a conversation with Steve Mathis in the Narthex. Steve was beginning to plan a work camp to Guatemala and had recently met with Roma Lee. He was, of course, quite enthusiastic about all the stories Roma Lee told him about work camps. He talked at great length about the miracles Roma Lee had witnessed and the wonderful stories she told.

Steve looked directly at me and said, "Bonnie, you are a writer. You should write her story."

I never thought about writing a biography. God would not let the thought leave my mind. I didn't sleep well that Sunday night, and all the next week, the words kept coming back to me, "You should write her story."

The next Sunday, I called Roma Lee and talked to her about writing her story so the miracles she witnessed and her stories of missions would not be lost.

Roma Lee politely said, "No, I don't think so. If someone writes about what I did, then it would take the glory from God."

I asked her to pray about the book. I was disappointed, of course, but felt if God wanted the book written, He would make a way. The next day, Roma Lee called me. She had talked to her daughters and they encouraged her to let me write her story. I am blessed God has given me this opportunity.

It has been my honor and privilege to know Roma Lee Courvisier as a woman of God, a work camp leader, and a friend. The time I have spent interviewing her has been precious to me. We often talked just as friends, the conversation interspersed with her marvelous stories of sixty-two years in ministry.

The first two chapters focus on the early days and are important in understanding the passion Roma Lee had for the poor and the lost, beginning with her salvation experience and continuing until today.

From there, the chapters are organized by country. In each of the chapters, I have written stories as told to me by Roma Lee. Each chapter also has newsletters written by her in a section titled "In Her Own Words," when newsletters are available. You, the reader, will feel the passion of her ministry in her own words as she tells the story of her journey.

Roma Lee frequently took her groups on side trips to enrich their understanding of the mission work at hand or the culture in which they were working. "A Side Trip" sections in this book give additional information about a particular country or mission work pertinent to the topic in the text.

The chapter "To the Next Generation" is a collection of writings from people whose lives and viewpoint of missions have been affected by Roma Lee's ministry.

This is an amazing story of a woman totally committed to Christ. She ministered to one person at a time, often finding the one person in a crowd who needed her help. She ministered to one group at a time to provide meaningful, life-changing experiences for each group she took with her. She poured her life into a lifestyle of missions, ever seeking the guidance of Christ in sharing the gospel one day at a time.

—Bonnie Newell

CHAPTER 1

Not Far from the Cotton Fields

As a child, Roma Lee lived in Elwood, Texas. A white, picturesque church sat beside a rural road; however, there was no pastor and no congregation. There was no town, no gas station and no post office. Occasionally, people would gather in the church to sing familiar hymns. As a child she sang songs such as "Rescue the Perishing" and "Send the Light" but had no idea of the meaning of the words. The words of the two songs found meaning in her heart and soul after she became a Christian.

Rescue the perishing, duty demands it!
Strength for thy labor, the Lord will provide;
Back to the narrow way, patiently win them,
Tell the poor wanderer a Savior has died.
Rescue the perishing, care for the dying;
Jesus is merciful, Jesus will save.[1]

Send the light, the blessed Gospel light;
Let it shine from shore to shore!

1. "Rescue the Perishing." Lyrics by Fanny Crosby.

Send the light, the blessed Gospel light;
Let it shine forevermore![2]

"Once, a lady came to the community and taught a Sunday school class for a few weeks," recalled Roma Lee. "She walked down the country roads inviting children to go with her. The children happily followed her." Roma Lee was nine or ten years old, but she never forgot the impact this initial exposure to Bible stories had on her life.

When Roma Lee was about twelve years old, she began to pick cotton in the fields near her home. She worked to earn money for school clothes each year. Once school started each fall, she did not work as many hours, but she would continue until the harvest was completed.

She shared, "I could pick more cotton than I could lift in a sack. Sometimes, I picked as much as four hundred pounds of cotton a day, and that did not include pulling the bolls off. Many men could not pick that much. I got a lot of attention as a child picking cotton." She picked cotton until she was about fifteen years old.

"I felt that I would never go very far from the cotton fields," related Roma Lee. But God had other plans for her life. Not only did she travel far away from the cotton fields of Texas, but she also ministered to countless numbers of people both in the United States and throughout the world as a result of her willingness to obey God.

Her parents moved from northeast Texas to west Texas when she was a junior in high school. They settled on a small farm near Abilene. Brother and Sister Ed Hunter visited up and down the sandy roads near Roma Lee's home inviting people to church. Not many would go with them, but they were persistent. Roma Lee was happy to go with them. Not only did the Hunters pick her up on Sundays but also for special services and other activities.

---

2. "Send the Light." Lyrics by Charles H. Gabriel.

Brother Hunter did not consider it a problem to drive miles and miles to pick up people and drive them to church in Abilene.

"I didn't have to hear the gospel very many times before I knew I wanted forgiveness and acceptance. I am so grateful that someone was out doing evangelism," recalled Roma Lee. Her parents were not Christian at the time, but they had very strong convictions about ethics and morals.

Kimbill and Eva Jean Young (Eva Jean was the Hunters' daughter) invited Roma Lee to their home nearly every Sunday along with others from the church. Roma Lee spent the afternoon with the Youngs, went to the evening service, and the Hunters took her home. Eva Jean was Roma Lee's spiritual mentor. The family relationships came full circle when David Young, the Youngs' son, accompanied Roma Lee on her last work camp prior to retirement.

Roma Lee worked on the family fruit farm. Customers filled the parking area and lined the country road. They sold peaches, apples, pears, blackberries, grapes, and pecans. She especially enjoyed meeting and greeting the customers.

One of her fondest memories of childhood was working at her uncle's farm supply store with her cousin May Glen Bigbee. The store's inventory included such items as animal feed, turkeys, eggs, and chickens, as well as other farm supplies. At times, the two would manage the store alone when her uncle had to be gone. She and her cousin embroidered when the store wasn't busy. "We were as happy as we could be. We would laugh and enjoy talking with the customers. Now kids are on their cell phones, but we just enjoyed each other's company," she says.

"My first choice was to go to college, but there was no money. I was happy staying with my parents and helping on the farm. I understood my parents' situation. I didn't know until many years later that my mom cried because she and Dad could not afford to send me to college, since I loved school."

Although Roma Lee did not have a formal college education, throughout her life she attended conferences and read many books. Study, prayer, and service helped her pursue her call to ministry.

Roma Lee met Frank Courvisier in church. After she and Frank were married on September 7, 1949, they returned to the church in Abilene as pastors.

"There were unreached people everywhere, even though there were a lot of churches and church schools in the area," recalled Roma Lee.

In Her Own Words

Holidays, 1998—Let's Celebrate!

I experienced the birth of Christ in my heart in 1947. I'm still celebrating!

The year 1998 has not been my best year health-wise. However, it has been a blessed year in ministry and rewards. God gave strength for several mission trips, and at this time my health continues to improve. I am excited as I look ahead to mission next year.

The year 1999 marks my 50th year in full-time Christian ministry (1949–1999), with thirty-one years as a pastor's wife and nineteen years in missions.

I am often asked questions about how I got started in mission work. It was more than fifty years ago when God began preparing me for a lifetime of ministry. It was 1948 and I was nineteen years of age. Even as a young Christian, I felt that missions began at home and kept reaching out.

My family lived on a small farm twelve miles from Abilene, Texas. I had heard about an area of Abilene where there were many children and families living without sufficient clothes, food or housing. I shared my concern for this need with my dear friend Alice Chapman. Then, and through the years, Alice has been a tremendous influence in my life. I asked Alice if she would go with me to begin a program of recreation, visitation and Sunday school in that community. Even though she (she says) was timid and afraid, she said, "Yes."

On Saturdays, we gave treats, lots of hugs and played games with the children and youth. Softball was the favorite game. Our Saturday uniforms were jeans and ball caps. Actually, Alice was the Home Run Queen. Each week, we visited every home in the community—sometimes giving food and clothes.

On Sunday morning, we taught classes for children and youth. Sometimes a parent would attend. After Sunday school, we would take some of the older ones to church service with us. A businessman provided a building for our classes and parties. Sometimes, businessmen donated treats and small gifts. Our home church donated bags of candy, fruit and nuts at Christmas time. The average class attendance the first month was 30. Saturday attendance was 40 to 60, depending on the weather. Sunday classes grew from 50 to 60.

There are always blessings received when we serve the Lord. Sometimes, there are those special rewards that last a lifetime. Such was a person that God brought into my life at the Abilene Mission. She was a tall, beautiful, soft-spoken teenager named Billy Jean. It was a joy to see her grow in the Lord, and then to see her develop into a leader of youth. Later, she became a devoted wife and mother. She also became an excellent teacher of children. Today, her life and faith continue to be an inspiration to me. We were ready for action with bags of treats for the children. Wow! You'd think that in more than fifty years, I'd have a new plan—something other than a bag of treats and lots of hugs!

The poor children in the homes in Abilene still represent needs in our community and world today. There is hope because hope was born on Christmas Day. Christ the Lord still changes lives.

Now, you know how it all began for me. You know the rest of the story.

Wishing you a Merry Christmas and a blessed new year.

Love, Roma Lee

A Side Trip

Picking Cotton

Picking cotton was difficult work. To pick cotton you must have a cotton sack ten to twelve feet long with a strap around your shoulder. In a bent over posture, you pluck the cotton that has blossomed out. You pick as many as both hands can hold and then put them into the sack. You have to wear gloves so that the dried bristles from the plant do not cut your fingers. Workers often go into the fields at 5:00 a.m. and work until 4:00-5:00 p.m. Cotton grows in hot climates, so workers are often in the fields with 100-degree temperatures. The white fluffy cotton fiber grows in a protective capsule called a boll. Before the cotton gin was invented by Eli Whitney in 1793, the boll and the seeds inside the fiber had to be removed by hand before the cotton could be of use.[3]

---

3. Alejomag, "How to Pick Cotton from the Fields," http://www.ehow.com/how_2183356_pick-cotton-fields.html.

Top: Roma Lee (right) and Alice Chapman (left) ready for ministry in Abilene.
Bottom: Billy Jean (left) and Roma Lee (right) ready to help in the community. Notice Roma Lee has a treat bag ready for the children.

Top: A home in the Abilene community
Bottom: Children in the community in Abilene, Texas where Roma Lee began her ministry as a teenager.

CHAPTER 2

Pastoral Ministry

Early Pastorates

The Courvisiers' first pastorate was a small congregation in Sweetwater, Texas, from 1949 to 1952.

"The church was small, but some of the best people in the world worshipped and served there," stated Roma Lee.

Most of the church ministries were for adults. An outreach ministry to children and youth was needed. "But how would we get them to church?" Roma Lee wondered.

An old milk delivery truck was purchased and converted into a vehicle to transport people to church. Benches were put in the truck, and so began a bus ministry plus children's and youth ministry.

The Courvisiers' second pastorate was in Abilene, Texas, from 1953 to 1957. This was the church were Roma Lee made her decision to be a Christian. It was there, even as a new Christian, that she felt the need to have a ministry to the poor and neglected. A program of visitation and recreation was a regular occurrence every Saturday. Sunday school was held every Sunday morning. Volunteers used their personal vehicles to pick up people who wanted to go to church after Sunday school.

Roma Lee remembered, "To be back in my home church and to continue ministries started earlier was a blessing indeed!"

The Courvisiers did evangelistic work in 1958 while serving as interim pastors in Sweetwater, Texas.

Pleasant Prairie Church of God

The Courvisiers' third pastorate was the Pleasant Prairie Church of God in Satanta, Kansas from 1959-1972.

Roma Lee recalled, "The church wasn't exactly in Satanta. The small town of Satanta was eighteen miles away. Shopping for groceries and other household supplies, taking the girls for piano lessons, and making hospital visits was thirty miles away in Garden City. I loved living the rural area. I loved every day with the people for those thirteen and a half years."

"It was the best place in the world to raise our daughters. Wheat fields and cattle surrounded the parsonage. The Pleasant Prairie people were wonderful, caring and giving people. They were always ready to help a neighbor or someone on the other side of the world."

There was a settlement of families with children several miles from the church. They worked at a gas plant named City Services. Roma Lee believed it was a perfect place for a bus ministry. She approached the church board about securing transportation for a bus ministry. One of the men in the congregation bought a big yellow school bus and the church bought another bus. The buses were used to bring people from the gas plant to church. The bus ministry also reached out to families in Satanta.

Roma Lee continued, "For most, the days of bus ministry have passed. Churches have moved on to better ways of outreach and communication. There are so many new ways to teach the old, old, story of Jesus. This is a wonderful day to be serving the Lord. I am glad I am able to see the amazing things God is doing in our world today. My passion for God's work is still the same as when I first began my walk with the Lord. At age eighty-four, my body is weak but my spirit still soars."

Some of the people who were young couples during their pastorate are still living in the area and now have grandchildren and great-grandchildren. The third generation is still serving the Lord in their community and in world missions.

On the occasions when she went back to speak at a church homecoming or missions convention, the children welcomed her as though they knew her. The Courvisiers were affectionately known at Pleasant Prairie as Brother and Sister Co.

Roma Lee enjoyed the role of counselor at youth camps. Her sense of humor followed her everywhere, especially at a youth camp. On one particular occasion, she was a counselor in one of the dormitories, which was a long metal building housing about forty girls.

An old abandoned building near the perimeter of the camp intrigued Roma Lee. One night after the girls had gotten settled for the night, Roma Lee presented an idea to the girls.

"Let's gather all of our belongings, suitcases, bed rolls, clothes...everything and take it to that old abandoned building. Wouldn't it be fun to see what the rest of the camp thinks when they wake up and we are gone?"

Of course, girls at camp are always ready for adventure and fun.

In the middle of the night under the cover of darkness, Roma Lee and the girls moved everything from the dormitory. There was nothing left behind, not even a tube of toothpaste, that would hint at anyone having ever been in the dormitory.

One can only imagine the mystery each camper and counselor tried to solve at breakfast the next morning when a whole dormitory of girls had apparently disappeared into thin air.

The girls could only imagine what questions the campers were whispering to each other, "Did someone kidnap them, did they all get sick, did they run away, did aliens come and take them? What could have happened to all of them at once?"

Then, appearing walking across the field, came Roma Lee followed by the girls and all of their belongings marching back to camp just in time for breakfast.

Roma Lee said she thought she might be in trouble with a stern lady preacher who was at the camp. "I wasn't afraid of snakes, but I was afraid of her." Roma Lee had actually told the camp director of her plan to have fun with the girls, but no one else knew. "It was fun and no one got hurt. When you have fun with people, you build relationships and trust. When people trust you, you can have serious conversations later on."

Mount Sterling, Kentucky

The Courvisiers went to Mt. Sterling in the winter of 1972 and left in December of 1980.

"I have always wanted to find people who needed the Lord, wherever they were," stated Roma Lee. "I believed in bus ministry before bus ministry was popular. Call it what you want, it was just a means to provide a way for people of all ages to attend church."

Roma Lee worked tirelessly in the bus ministry at Mt. Sterling. At one time, there were more than two hundred fifty people riding the buses to church. The people included children, youth, and adults.

"When Frank and I left Mt. Sterling, many of the leaders in the youth group were children who started coming on the buses years before," shared Roma Lee.

"I can remember my heart just bursting with love for the youth since I had seen them grow up. When they were young children, I would go to their doors and even inside their houses to pick them up for church.

"If I heard a voice in the house say, 'The kids aren't dressed, they can't go to church today.'

I replied, 'Oh, let me help you get them dressed.'"

She would proceed to go into the house and get the children ready for church.

At first, children and youth came to church on the bus. Later, entire families came in their own cars. Eventually, most of the drivers of the four church buses were fathers of children who first came to church on the buses.

"Bus ministry served the poor as well as those who had the comforts of life. When you bring in four busloads of children, you are stretching the boundaries. I made sure there were programs for them. Walls can be repainted, but children can't be replaced." said Roma Lee.

The Mt. Sterling church purchased a new bus because the number of those riding the bus continued to grow. One of the little boys who had been riding the bus was hit and killed by a car. There was no other church connection for his parents other than that he went to church on the bus. The parents became Christians after losing their son. The boy's father then became a bus driver for the church.

Roma Lee states, "Someone took me to church before my parents went to church. There are children who will go to church if someone will go and get them. Then their parents will come to church and hear the gospel. God did not intend for the little boy to be run over by a car, but through the tragedy, the family came to church, became Christian and then church leaders."

There were two houses of prostitution on the bus routes. A mother and her three daughters lived in one of the houses. Roma Lee believed that anyone who was willing go to church should be welcome in church. "Everyone needs to hear the gospel," she stated.

"I started waving to the girls and the mother as I passed their house. Later, I would just say a few words and be friendly. Soon, I sat on the front porch of their house and visited with them. It wasn't long before they came to church with me."

There was a second house of prostitution that she often passed. "The yard was fenced in, so I would just go and hang out by the fence and talk to the girls."

One young girl about sixteen years old particularly touched her heart. After a time of getting to know the girl through fence conversations, she asked, "Will you ride the bus to church with me?"

The girl replied, "Oh, I can't go to church. I don't have anything to wear; I don't have clothes good enough to wear to church."

Roma Lee promptly took clothing to the girl. The madam of the house did not want the girl separated from her. She somehow knew that Roma Lee's influence would lead the girl away from the house. Consequently, the madam started riding the bus and attending church. Even at church, the madam did not want the young girl to be separated from her, but Roma Lee would take the woman to a Sunday school class and tell her, "I know you will enjoy this class!" Roma Lee took the girl to her office and talked and prayed with her.

On one day, Roma Lee took clothes to the girl and found the gate unlocked. She proceeded to the door and knocked. The madam answered the door and hesitated to let Roma Lee inside the house. Roma Lee just kept smiling and talking as she walked into the house.

"Where is Cindy's room?[1] I want to give her these clothes," asked Roma Lee.

The madam replied, "I'll give them to her. You don't need to go to her room."

1. The girl's name has been changed to protect her.

"Please, where is her room? I want to give them to her personally."

"It's down there," said the madam pointing to a hallway.

At that moment, a man came out of one of the rooms. He looked familiar. Roma Lee could not recall his name exactly but she knew that he was a businessman in town.

The gentleman nervously said, "I'm here to look at some photo albums."

Roma Lee was positive that the man recognized her. The madam looked anxious about the encounter. Roma Lee, trying to change the subject until she could find the young girl, said, "That is a beautiful basket," as she gestured to a nearby basket.

The madam quickly spoke, "Please, take the basket, it's yours!"

Roma Lee pushed past the gentleman and the madam in search of the young girl in her room. She found the teenage girl in a filthy room, sleeping on a worn out, dirty mattress on the floor. She noticed a huge hole in the door, most likely made by an angry customer. After giving Cindy the clothing, Roma Lee sat on the dirty mattress with her.

While sitting on the mattress, they heard a man's deep voice, "Who is that in there with you?"

Roma Lee simply replied, "I'm a friend."

One day, Roma Lee was again standing at the fence talking with Cindy. She knew Cindy had run away from home; she was afraid to go home, but afraid to stay in the current situation. A strange look came over Cindy's face as a car stopped in the street.

Roma Lee asked, "Do you know who's in that car?"

"It's my mom and dad," replied Cindy.

"Honey, run. Go now, run. Jump in the car and go with them. You must run now," urged Roma Lee.

Cindy ran and got into the car with her parents. Roma Lee never saw her again. Roma Lee noted, "I still have that basket in my living room to remind me my days of sharing the gospel with the prostitutes."

Glen Eden Retreat was in the mountains of Kentucky and used for youth camps. The camp could only accommodate one hundred youth plus counselors. Every space was always full. Roma Lee went as a counselor, but most who knew her also knew that she was in charge of mischief!

On one particular night, Roma Lee was very strict with the girls and wanted everyone in bed early. "Let's get into bed, girls. Time to get settled. Leave the windows open tonight. It is very hot and we will need the air circulation."

The girls' dorm was an old abandoned school building with the windows facing the cemetery. Roma Lee's cot was just outside the door of the girls' room.

This particular night, after insisting the girls go to bed early, she tied the door closed with a strip of sheet cut from her own bed sheet. She silently slipped out into the cemetery with a tape player in hand. She had purchased a cassette tape of a man with a deep voice laughing and rerecorded it so that the deep voice played over and over. As she played the tape, Roma Lee could hear the girls screaming and trying to open the door of their room.

Lynette, Roma Lee's daughter, was one of the campers that night. Roma Lee heard her say, "It's ok, it's ok, girls. It's probably just my mom doing something."

When Frank became ill and could no longer pastor, Roma Lee began taking work camps overseas more frequently. She stated, "When I was no longer a pastor's wife, my mission just changed location. I went from working mostly in the local pastorate to working in other countries. I always felt missions was getting the gospel to people. My passion for the gospel didn't change, just my location."

In Her Own Words

This letter was written on the back of bank deposit slips. Susan Shotton Turner discovered it among Ruth Shotton's belongings after her death in 2010. This letter was written during the time the Courvisiers were pastors at Pleasant Prairie Church of God in Kansas.

Dear Ronald, Ruth and Family,

Did you ever see such writing paper? I'm in the hospital waiting room and have nothing else to write on. Bro. Co. (Frank Courvisier) is in visiting Arthur Alexander now. He just visited Grandpa Shotton. It is not visiting hours so he found him alone. Grandpa Shotton asked Bro. Co. to tell him a story, so he told him the story of Christ's coming and the message of salvation. Mr. Shotton said he had been saved as a child but had gotten away from the Lord. Bro. Co. explained the way back to Christ. They prayed together. It seemed that as best as he knew how, he was putting his trust in the Lord. He feels now that everything is all right. Just wanted to let you know this. Thought it would be an encouragement to you.

Ruth, we do hope you are feeling much better and can be home with the family at Christmas. Our thoughts and prayers are with you all.

Love, Sr. Co.

A Side Trip

Roma Lee and Frank lived in rural Kansas while pastoring the Pleasant Prairie Church of God. On the rural mail routes, you could send mail without a stamp to someone who was "upstream" from you or further on the route. If you wrote the words "Please leave today" on the letter for the letter carrier, then the recipient would get the letter on the same day you mailed it. Roma Lee recalled when she and Frank were considering leaving one pastorate for another, they were very open with the congregation and asked the congregation for their prayers in making the decision as to whether to stay at the current pastorate or move on to the next pastorate. The following is a story by Gary Taton of the time when Frank and Roma Lee were considering leaving Pleasant Prairie.

Leave Today!

It was a most glorious period of time having Frank and Roma Lee Courvisier as leaders of the Pleasant Prairie Church of God. Strong family ties were experienced during those fourteen years between pastor and community. It was a sad day indeed when Bro. Co. announced to the congregation that he was struggling with what he felt was the Lord's call to ministry in Mt. Sterling, Kentucky. Obedience to the Lord was his only choice and he asked the congregation to join with him in praying and fasting concerning this call. At the end of the two weeks of seeking God's direction, he wanted the members of the congregation to write him a letter expressing what each felt the Lord was telling them.

Like most folks in the community, my mother Erma Taton was devastated by the thought of losing Bro. Co. and his family, making it difficult to pray and easy to procrastinate in getting a letter written. She put if off as long as she could and finally got it written, but it was Saturday and Bro. Co. wanted the letters by Sunday. With the rural mail delivery, if you lived "up-stream" on the mail route and wanted a letter delivered that day, it was common practice to simply state so on the envelope, otherwise, it would be taken to the post office and not be delivered until the next day.

As Roma Lee brought Saturday's mail in from the parsonage mailbox, she exclaimed, "Well, Frank, here's our answer!"

Frank looked up quite puzzled because he could see that she was holding up an unopened envelope. As she got closer, he saw in extremely bold lettering, triple underscored:

PLEASE LEAVE TODAY!!

CHAPTER 3

Mexico

While Frank and Roma Lee were pastors of the Pleasant Prairie Church of God in Satanta, Kansas, they traveled to Mexico to visit Ron and Ruth Shotton. The purpose of the trip was to observe firsthand the needs of the work in Mexico then return to Kansas to raise needed funds. At that time, the church in Kansas gave one-half of the Shottons' financial support. Roma Lee and Frank believed it was important to keep the church updated on missionaries' needs.

The church in Saltillo, Mexico, was built primarily with funds from the Kansas church. When parishioner Edith Sprunger died, an offering was taken at her funeral service. The offering, plus money given by the church, was used to build the Saltillo church. The commitment of the Pleasant Prairie church was so strong that fifty people from the Pleasant Prairie Church attended the dedication service for the Saltillo church and Frank preached the dedication sermon.

As Roma Lee and Frank were walking in a Mexican village with Ruth and Ron, she saw a woman holding a small child in her arms. Ron said, "Her child is dying of malnutrition. All of the woman's children have died from starvation, and this child will not live long." As the result of a drought, the staple foods of corn and beans were scarce.

In years to come, Roma Lee could not get the picture of the mother and baby out of her mind. She knew that this mother was not the only mother suffering and losing children from the tragedy of starvation. Roma Lee recalled, "This was the first time that I saw true poverty. The needs of the poor touched my heart, and I have always remembered that day throughout my ministry as both a pastor's wife and a missionary. My heart has been tender toward the poor, whether in the States or in other countries."

At dusk, Roma Lee and Frank walked the dusty roads to a village for evening worship. Donkeys were braying and dogs barking. Once in a while a pig or chicken would scamper in or out of a house. Roma Lee saw smoke coming out of the tops of the houses. The curling smoke was evidence that the women were cooking the daily tortillas for the evening meal.

In the hour before church service, they enjoyed walking, visiting and playing with the children. A woman ran to the Shottons and the Courvisiers to give a gift of tortillas to the missionaries.

Roma Lee turned to Ruth and said, "I can't accept these tortillas; I know that this is all she has to feed her family tonight."

"We must accept her gift or she will think it is not good enough for us," Ruth quickly responded.

From that day, throughout her ministry, Roma Lee remembered the advice of Ruth and graciously accepted gifts without question.

As Roma Lee and Frank continued to travel the dusty roads, they noticed a couple and a small child with a donkey-drawn cart. The cart held the precious contents of a bucket of water. A heavy rain had provided water for their family. Ron drew their attention to the many houses in village after village dotting the countryside in the distance.

"The gospel has not yet been taken to those villages," Ron shared with a heavy heart. Roma Lee's heart was saddened and burdened by the thought that so many people had not heard the gospel.

Later, Roma Lee entered a small house in one of the little villages that had a fire burning on a dirt floor both for cooking and for warmth. A little *abuela* (grandma) was sitting on a handmade stool, crocheting around the edges of a table cover that she had made in the dark room with only the fire for light.

Roma Lee said, "This is a beautiful tablecloth, may I buy it from you?"

Abuela responded, " Oh no, it is not finished yet. See, this part is not done."

Roma Lee asked again, "I would like to buy your beautiful work even though it is not finished." The abuela agreed to sell the tablecloth.

"The smell of the smoke from the darkly lit room in the remote village in Mexico remained in the cloth for years," Roma Lee said. "When I would get the cloth out of my cupboard, the smell would remind me of Mexico as I would pray for the needs of the people in all of the little villages dotting the countryside and that they would know Jesus."

Some years later, Roma Lee took a group to Mexico to build a pastor's home. Dr. Gil Wagoner, a medical doctor, accompanied the group to provide much needed medical help to the poor in the villages.

"Roma Lee, when will the people come? Do the people know that we are having a clinic today?" questioned Dr. Wagoner.

"Dr. Wagoner, please just get out everything that you brought. Get out your supplies, medicine, and all of the equipment that you brought with you," responded Roma Lee.

Dr. Wagoner said, "But Roma Lee, there are no people here. When will they come?"

"My Spanish is not the best, but I will go into the village and tell people that a doctor is here."

As she went from street to street, she invited them to come, "If anyone is sick, please come. We have a doctor here. Is anyone sick, do you have family members who are sick? Come and see the doctor."

The people lined up at the makeshift clinic. Using his bilingual skills, Dr. Wagoner tended to the medical needs of patient after patient. Dr. Wagoner was thrilled so many people had come for medical help. He had asked the Lord for one special thing. He asked that he might be able to lead at least one person to Christ each day. On the very first day, a husband and wife accepted Christ as their Savior.

Finally Dr. Wagoner said, "Roma Lee, you have to stop going into the village and getting people. We have enough patients to treat for now."

The work campers brought a large supply of medicines, so Dr. Wagoner had the supplies needed to treat hundreds of patients during the five days while the remainder of the work campers completed building the pastor's home.

Dr. Wagoner recalled when he was with Roma Lee at the Mexico-United States border, the group was quite nervous about the border guards discovering the items in the trunk of the vehicle. He recalled they waited for an hour for the guards to inspect the car in front of them. The guards searched every person thoroughly, as well as the trunk, wheel-wells, under the hood, behind the seats, and every inch, it seemed, of the car.

Dr. Wagoner recalled that Roma Lee simply said, "Pray, just pray."

The precious cargo in the trunk was clothing for the poor and a great deal of medicine for Dr. Wagoner's clinics. The border guards would not have let the medicines pass the checkpoint, had they found them.

As the work campers' car pulled up for their turn at the checkpoint, the guard waved them through without any inspection of the vehicle or the passengers in the vehicle. A miracle? Indeed!

Roma Lee visited another home when a mother was putting her children to bed. The children had boards to keep them off the dirt floor, but no mattress, sheets or pillows.

She recalled, "I never felt the same when I was home and putting my girls to bed. I appreciated that I had beds, sheets, and pillows for my children. As I tucked in my children, I could see in my mind the little village in Mexico with the mother putting her children to sleep on boards."

The images of poverty are indelibly etched on the hearts of those who are sensitive to the needs of others. Roma Lee is an example of one who never forgets the images and in turn becomes the hands of Christ to help those in need.

Work campers building a a home for a pastor in Mexico.

CHAPTER 4

Panama

Dean and Nina Flora were the missionaries in Panama when Roma Lee and Frank pastored the Pleasant Prairie Church of God in Kansas. Roma Lee recalled with fondness the trips to Panama and the San Blas Islands. The purpose of the trips was to experience firsthand the needs of the missionaries and then return home to raise money.

Roma Lee recalled with a smile, "Dean Flora was the best storyteller ever." One story in particular, inspired, impacted and challenged her.

Dean had a passion for sharing the gospel with the Kuna Indians and was instrumental in sharing the gospel for the first time with many of them. As Dean was leaving one of the San Blas Islands in a boat, he saw a boat coming toward him with a Kuna man standing in the boat waving his arms frantically.

As the boat drew closer, the man said, "Are you Dean Flora?"

Dean, not knowing the intent of the man's question answered a little cautiously, "Yes, I am."

The Kuna man responded, "I have just one question, does God really have a Son?"

Dean, of course replied, "Yes, God really *does* have a Son."

The Kuna then inquired, "When are you going to come to my island and tell us about God's Son?"

"Many people assume everyone has heard the gospel," stated Roma Lee. "The people of the San Blas Islands, the jungle, and many others on the mainland of Panama had not heard the gospel."

"When are you going to come to my island and tell us about God's Son?" is a question that burns in the heart of Roma Lee and many others who have a passion to share the good news with those who have not heard. Roma Lee visited ten of the 378 San Blas Islands during her time in Panama. She continued to visit the islands for many years after Frank was unable to go.

To travel to the islands, one must travel by boat or small plane. The small jungle planes would not accommodate but a few at a time. Part of the group would travel by plane and the rest would wait on the mainland for the plane to return and take a few more people.

One particular occasion, a group made up mostly of teenagers needed three trips to get them all to the island. The islands are small and it was always a memorable experience to land and take off with very short runway. It was a nail-biting experience to gauge whether the small plane would actually get into the air before it plunged into the sea.

Roma Lee, her daughter Lee Ann, and a few teenagers went on the first flight. Adult chaperones were left for each of the other two plane trips. The Kuna women wear a dark line down the nose and a gold ring in the nose as a traditional marking.

Roma Lee asked Dean, "Why do the ladies wear the black line down their nose?" She was anticipating some traditional story that had lasted for generations.

Dean replied, "Why do women put black on their eyelids in the United States? It is just pretty!"

Roma Lee, with a mischievous look in her eye, turned to the ladies in the group and said, "Let's put a black line on our noses like the Kuna women."

Of course, the girls agreed and were prepared to greet the next two planes resembling the Kuna women. The Kuna women have a great sense of humor and were happy to provide Kuna blouses and headscarves to the girls. The mixture used to paint the beauty mark on the nose is similar to a permanent dye. Not only did the girls greet their fellow work campers with the nose marking, but some greeted their families upon return to the States with a faint marking still on their nose.

The Kuna women are very active, taking care of their thatched-roof homes, children, and cooking, as well as making the beautiful Mola blouses. On one trip, the women were busy cooking fish on an open fire for dinner. The fish were very black with the eyes still looking at the consumer when they were served.

Roma Lee remembered, "I sat there looking at that very black fish looking back at me and knew that I had to eat it since it had so graciously been prepared for me." She always tried to eat the food of the people she visited and this was no exception.

On another occasion, the women were cooking something resembling spaghetti in large black pots on an open fire. Roma Lee was fascinated with an animal tied with a rope near the cooking pots. It was the size of a small dog but looked more like a large rat. When the food was served, there was meat in the spaghetti and the animal near the pots had mysteriously disappeared.

Roma Lee remembered, "I didn't feel that the meat in the spaghetti was unsafe; after all, it had been cooked!"

Not all of the food was questionable as to its origins; one meal was lobster the men caught in the crystal-clear, blue ocean waters surrounding the island. That meal was delectable!

Dean shared with Roma Lee, "Once the chief of an island becomes a Christian, then most of the people follow the example of their chief." He continued to work tirelessly to share the gospel with the Kuna.

Roma Lee remembered, "It was not only sharing the gospel and the Kuna accepting Christ, but it was training and discipleship that took so much time. The Kuna had never heard the gospel or read the Bible. I was in Panama when the Bible in the Kuna language was delivered to Dean. It was an exciting time!"

Work campers slept in the large community building in hammocks, the only bed the Kuna use. The building had a thatched roof and bamboo walls.

Roma Lee recalled, "The work campers were provided with candles in cans to provide light. At night, you could see eyes peeking through the bamboo walls. I'm sure it was interesting to watch the North Americans try to get used to sleeping in hammocks. Sometimes getting into the hammock without being flipped over was the first challenge."

In the 1980s, Roma Lee and one other woman visited one of the San Blas Islands. "The Kuna women were good leaders. The women's group had a president. Often, she was in charge of housing and food for guests as was the case this night. Three hammocks were hung in a small thatched roof church."

Roma Lee thought, "One hammock for my friend, one for the president, and one for me." Much to her surprise, the pastor of the church was the third person sleeping in the church that night right beside her hammock.

In the morning, from her viewpoint at the church, Roma Lee watched the village come alive. Ladies made fires for cooking, scurried to get ready for a day with visitors, and filling the air were the noises of children as they awakened. This was truly a paradise. The Kuna women often do not wear blouses because it is hot on the islands. That morning, it was no different.

Roma Lee was relieved when the pastor was up early and left the church. Thinking she was safe, she began to put on a clean blouse; the pastor came dashing back into the church, hopped on the hammock, thinking nothing of it. A way of life that has survived generation after generation is not changed by the visit of a few foreigners.

Kuna bathrooms provided a unique experience. A platform sat on stilts over the ocean with a wooden shed of sorts built on the platform. The slats of the shed were far apart and one easily saw into the shed. Everything from the bathroom washed onto the beach. With no other choices, work campers experienced everyday life on the San Blas Islands.

Roma Lee always felt safe on the San Blas Islands. If a Kuna committed a crime, the punishment was severe. As a result, they did not break their communal laws. She could leave her purse or any other belongings anywhere on the island and they would not be touched.

The Kuna used coconuts as money and kept them in coconut banks. Trading ships came to the islands and the Kuna traded coconuts for cloth and other items they needed.

Due to bad weather, one of Roma Lee's groups was not able to leave the islands in the normal way on small planes. A trading ship neared the islands; the group boarded it to go back to the mainland. Although the waters were rough and many in the group became ill due to the rough seas, the group arrived safely back to the Panama mainland and continued their mission.

Roma Lee and Frank both had a passion to raise awareness of the missionaries' needs and subsequently raise funds. Their passion for missions spilled over into the lives of the people they pastored. Leslie Alexander and his wife Olive attended the Pleasant Prairie Church of God. Both accompanied the Courvisiers on trips to Panama and Guatemala. Leslie decided to take out a life insurance policy specifically to go to missions. Soon after, he was diagnosed with cancer but wanted to go on one more mission trip. Although in pain, he and Olive visited the mission work in Panama and Guatemala.

The river in Panama was the lifeline of the jungle work for the Floras. The indigenous people traveled by small boats to gathering places and stayed the weekend for church services. At the time of Leslie's visit, there were not enough boats to transport all the people to church services.

In Guatemala, he visited the "Church of the Widows." The name came from an incident involving terrorists who put all the men of the village inside the church building and the women and children outside the building. The terrorists then proceeded to burn the building with the men inside while the women and children were forced to watch. The church rose again through the help of Juan Cadel, a Guatemalan evangelist. Juan needed a motorcycle for his ministry.

After Leslie Alexander passed from this earthly life, his family carried out his wishes and used the life insurance money to purchased boats for Dean Flora's jungle ministry and a motorcycle for Juan Cadel's ministry. Since that time, the children and grandchildren of the Alexanders have gone on mission's trips with Roma Lee. The passion for missions has passed from one generation to the next. Two of the Alexanders' grandchildren are career missionaries.

A Side Trip

Kuna Indians

The Kuna Indians are a tribe in Panama numbering approximately 35,000. They speak their own language called Tule. Many Kuna speak Spanish and some speak English. The Kuna women wear wraparound skirts and beautifully hand-made blouses known as Molas. The Mola is an intricately sewn picture made from layers of cloth in a reverse appliqué technique. The men wear a traditional Kuna shirt and less traditional pants, jeans, or shorts. Kuna women also paint their faces with homemade rouge made from achiote seeds. They usually wear a nose ring and paint a line down their nose.

The Kuna have plots of land in the jungle on Panama's mainland where they grow plantain, bananas, avocados, corn and some tuber plants like manioc. They eat a variety of wild game hunted from the jungle but their staples are fish (Tilapia) and plantain. Their principle drink is corn boiled in water.

They have the most advanced political system of any tribal group in Latin America. They have three chiefs who manage village politics and a series of meetings called *congresos*.[1]

1. Adapted from Eddie L. Bowerman, "About the Kuna Indians," http://public.cwpanama.net/~bowerman/page3.html.

Roma Lee (far left) and work campers dressed in traditional Kuna clothing.

CHAPTER 5

Costa Rica

Work camps must always have a few rules. Helping the group members realize the importance of keeping the rules remains the discretion of the leader. On one occasion, in a group meeting, Roma Lee discussed the seriousness of keeping rules.

Roma Lee informed two young men, "If you do not keep the rules, you will have to eat chicken feet soup. That's how things are done in Costa Rica."

Later that day, Roma Lee made the daily trip to the local market to purchase items needed for the vegetable soup for the evening meal. She also purchased a surprise ingredient for the two young men.

When she arrived back at the home, she quietly said to a few of the girls in the group, "Come, help me prepare the evening meal." She produced two chicken feet she had purchased in the market. "Here, use this polish and paint the toenails of the chicken's feet. We need it for our evening meal."

The girls willingly assisted Roma Lee with the nail-polishing task while the cooks prepared a delicious vegetable soup for the entire group. Roma Lee quietly instructed the cooks, "When you serve the soup to the work campers tonight, put a chicken foot on top of the soup for each of the two young men."

One can just hear the stifled giggles of the cooks, the girls, and Roma Lee as they prepared to serve the soup. One can only imagine the surprised facial expression of the two young men when they were served chicken-foot vegetable soup, all the time wondering what rule they could have possibly broken to have this kind of punishment!

In Her Own Words

Roma Lee wrote this story in 2012 to share her experiences in Costa Rica.

I started going to Costa Rica in 1981. That was the year I started sponsoring a six-year-old girl, Rosaura Espinoza Rodriquez. I sponsored her until she was married.

In 1982, when I was in Costa Rica, I spent a night in the home of Rosaura and her family. Their house was small, furnishings simple, a cement slab on the back porch for washing, no indoor bath, a small wood-burning stove for cooking, and a little corner cupboard for dishes. Everything, including the wooden floors, was spotless. I was blessed to be in this home where I was welcomed and loved. We all sang hymns together—they sang in Spanish and I sang in English. After songs and prayers, Rosaura's mother made hot chocolate for us.

The next morning, Rosaura's father was up at 4:00 a.m. preparing to leave for work in the sugar cane fields. He worked six days a week for $10.00. Before I left, I was served a breakfast of black beans and rice.

For eleven years, I led many work camps to Costa Rica. Work campers worked with nationals to build many churches. It was exciting to see the zeal of the Christians. New Christians would start churches in communities even when there was no building for worship. I remember worshipping with Christians just starting a church in the village of Altos de Peralta. They had no church building, no property on which to build, and no funds to buy property. The service was held on the porch of a home. The speaker and the singers stood on the porch. People came from every direction. They filled the yard; some were standing on a hillside and others in the street. Many came to hear the gospel for the first time.

On another trip to Costa Rica, all work campers stayed with Christian families. My daughter, Lee Ann, was with me. We both stayed with Rosaura and her family. After the service at the church, we were sitting with our family. Rosaura and her brother, Marlon were singing when the house started to move. The house was rolling from side to side. It was what they called, a rolling earthquake. Nails began to come out of the wooden walls. Rosaura and Marlon never moved from where they were sitting. They stopped singing and I could hear their sweet voices in prayer. There was a new baby in the family and I was holding the baby. Rosaura's mother put her arms around both the baby and me. I could hear her praying softly. There was no panic just peace in the room. No one was hurt.

In Latin America, two of the most special events for a girl are her fifteenth birthday and her wedding. No matter how poor a family is, they will sacrifice to make these times very special for a daughter.

When I was preparing for any missions trip, God always provided just what we needed. As I was preparing for a trip to Costa Rica, someone asked me if I knew anyone in Latin America who needed a wedding dress. I ask the size. It was exactly Rosaura's size. I knew she had a boyfriend and this beautiful wedding gown would be perfect for her when she did marry.

I took the dress and told Rosaura, "This does not mean you need to marry soon, but when you do, you will have this beautiful dress."

The next time I was in Costa Rica, the wedding was already planned and I was to be the matron of honor. What an experience it was to shop in Latin America for a suitable dress for a North American woman to wear to a Latin wedding. Of course, it all worked out fine. No one cared what I wore anyway.

It was a beautiful wedding. After the vows were said, the bride and groom sat in chairs in front of the minister. The minister preached for at least an hour or more. This seemed to be a Latin custom.

There will forever be a special place in my heart for the people of Costa Rica.

CHAPTER 6

Guatemala

Roma Lee thoroughly enjoyed visiting the small villages in Guatemala. On one such visit with Shaney Calderon, wife of Isai Calderon, she and a group of young people arrived at dinnertime. They noticed the women were busy cooking dinner. The smell of the meal permeated their senses and the young people were very excited for the opportunity to taste local cuisine. As the meal was served, the excitement waned when chicken feet were floating on the top of the broth.

In quiet whispers, one could hear the group members asking each other, "Do we have to eat the chicken feet?"

After a short conversation between Shaney and Roma Lee, Shaney stated, "I'll just take care of it."

Roma Lee recalled the chicken feet mysteriously disappeared and no one knew exactly what happened to them. A collective sigh of relief hovered in the room. Roma Lee, as always, had her bag of goodies for just such an occasion. The work campers had a two-course dinner that night, a taste of the local delicacies and peanut butter crackers.

The Pleasant Prairie Church of God in Kansas supported the Calderons in the early 1970s. As was their custom, Roma Lee and Frank took a few parishioners to Guatemala to experience the needs firsthand. Then they would return to the church to raise funds to send to the missionaries to further the work of the church.

Roma Lee also recalled that while she was staying with the Calderons, an earthquake shook the countryside. The rolling of the earth and shaking of the house did not deter either her or the missionaries from their resolve to serve the needs of the people in Name of Jesus.

In Her Own Words

January 24, 1990—Antigua, Guatemala

My Prayer

Lord, I've just been sitting here in the quietness of the night, thinking about You, your Word, and the events of the day. You said that when we have visited the sick, fed the hungry, and loved the least of your children, we have done it unto You.

And I remember the words of the Apostle Paul when he said, "Don't forget to be kind to strangers, for some who have done this have entertained angels without realizing it" (Hebrews 13:2).

Lord, was it really You I fed today when I sat on the floor at the hospital and fed helpless little Christiana? When I first looked into her eyes, as she lay in the hospital bed, were they really your pleading eyes saying, "Help me"? She tried so hard to reach her arms up to me. When I lifted her up in my arms, spoke softly to her, and loved her, I could see the response in her eyes and she smiled. A nurse handed me a bowl of soup and bread. The soup was too hot, so I kept stirring it to cool it. Christiana was so hungry—her little mouth was open and she began to make noises as if to say, "Please hurry." She ate every bit of the food. Was it you Lord that I cradled in my arms today, or did I hold and feed an angel and not realize it?

As I visited room after room of helpless children (most of them orphans or abandoned), I looked into their brown eyes and realized they *all* had your eyes, Lord!

I saw six-year-old William lying on the floor. He couldn't even sit up. His legs are as helpless as if he were a rag doll. He is a bright and smiling little boy and was more than willing to talk with me. William will always live at the hospital because there is no one to care for him. His parents brought him there four years ago and never returned to visit him again.

Five-year-old Moa couldn't walk, but he crawled over to me and pulled himself up. I helped him on my lap and we looked at a book. When he thought he was losing my attention, he would say, "Mama, Mama," and start pointing at the pictures.

Soledad wasn't crying today as she often does. I wonder if every day she remembers the time the terrorists came to her little home in the mountains and killed her mother, father, brothers and sisters. She is so alone and sad. But today when she saw me, she smiled, waved, and threw me a kiss right off her little brown hand. Be near her, Lord Jesus, and bless her today.

How precious have been the hours spent with you today, Lord. Help me never to forget how you came to me through the "least of these," your children. May I always see this world, the hungry, hurting hearts, as though I were looking through your eyes—or as though I were looking into your eyes. Amen.

Roma Lee

October 1990—Antigua, Guatemala

Dear One,

Come walk with me…

As darkness wraps itself around the village like a soft velvet cloak, small open fires burn along the *calle* (street). Old women with leathery, wrinkled skin, bare feet and toothless smiles, roast corn over the fires. Small children sleep huddled near buildings covered with rags. There are men drunk with cheap liquor. They lay on the walkways and cobblestone streets. They have tried to escape their burdens, pain and fears. But when the day dawns tomorrow and the sun shines warm on the cobblestone, they will awaken to the same burdens. One woman sits on the edge of the sidewalk with the head of her drunken husband cradled in her lap, and there she will keep watch through the night. Oh, that they might know Him in whom is life. There is the soft patter of bare feet on the cobblestone as weary women travel homeward after long hours of sitting in the marketplace selling various wares. Baskets carried on their heads are filled with fruits, vegetables, blouses, blankets, *y muchas cosas* (and many things). Most of them carry a baby on their back. Some of them cradle a nursing baby in their arms.

I long to reach out in His name and touch them. To walk beside them or to stoop and wash their weary feet.

My gift of food to one is accepted as His gift given through me. As I walk beside her and carry part of her heavy load, I soon feel her weariness in my body. As we walk in silence, our hearts whisper what cannot be spoken.

Tomorrow, we will each walk alone, but we will be stronger because today we walked together.

Christ prayed that we might be one, that we *all* might be one. Even so Lord, let the answer begin in me.

For truly we are one...

In the Bond of Love,
Roma Lee

January, 1991—Guatemala

We were almost to Cantel, the Indian village at the foot of the mountains near the city of Quetzaltenago.

Many Indian people were walking along the roadside, mostly women and children. It was late afternoon, time for mothers to be home cooking tortillas on the hot stones over an open fire. The women in bright dress carrying baskets on their heads, a baby on their back with bare feet were hurrying toward home.

And then it happened...

Just ahead of our vans, a car hit a small child. The child was dead instantly. The body still lying in the road was covered with a white sack. From under the covering extended the arm and hand of a small child in a pool of blood. Pain and sorrow gripped our hearts and tears filled our eyes. The face was covered but that small hand looked like the hand of our child or grandchild back home. It looked like the hands that had reached out to us and held onto us in villages and churches. The picture of that small hand will forever be imprinted on our minds and hearts. But the picture that will perhaps be the clearest and most painful will be the agony and grief on the face of the mother as she knelt on the ground, lifting her arms and crying out for help.

In that moment, if it would have been possible, no sacrifice would have been too great if we could have given life to that child and placed it in the mother's arms. We would have gladly worked or given the last dollar in our pockets if in so doing we could have given life.

We could do nothing to give life back to the dead child lying in the road, but that small lifeless hand can be a reminder to all of us of the little hands around the world who reach out to us, little children to whom we may give life. We can give, we can go, we can work, and we can pray that they may receive the Word of God, that they may hear of Jesus, that they may feel His love, truly know, and believe that salvation, hope, and life are through Jesus Christ, not the witchdoctor. We can build churches and schools where the children can receive Christian training. We can give the gift of life when we give the Word of God.

If the death of that one child, that one small outstretched hand, can cause us to make a deeper commitment of our lives to a life-giving ministry, then that one precious child will not have died in vain.

Roma Lee

January 1991

The sun was hot and work was hard as the North American work team build a second floor educational unit to the church in Coban, Guatemala.

The heat, sunburned skin, blistered hands and aching backs did not keep the sounds of joyous laughter and songs of praise from ringing forth as a witness to the community that truly there is joy in the service of the Lord.

Cultures blended, hearts bonded in love, forever friendships were formed, and God poured out His Spirit upon us. Very quickly the new building went up.

In Coban, there is now a place where children can receive Christian education and the total church ministry be expanded because of people who are willing to say, "Here am I Lord, send me."

When the work on the building site was completed, we moved on to other locations to share in services. We were blessed and the churches encouraged as work campers preached, sang and gave testimonies of their experiences with the Lord. The greatest of blessings was to see some along the way receive Christ as Savior

We shall never forget the scene and experience in the community of Delores. We arrived at the church on Monday evening (not a regular church service night). We arrived over an hour before service time. We wanted time to visit in homes and give clothes to these very needy people. The people work gathering coffee beans, often earning less than $1.00 a day. Even though we arrived early, many people were already at the church. The people continued to come, some walking for miles to attend the service.

The church filled—and still the people came. The North American men were asked to sit or stand on the platform—and still the people came. The children were asked to fill the front of the church and sit on the floor—and still the people came. The aisles were filled—and still the people came. When there was no more room inside, many stood in the doorway and in the yard. One man, who was unable to get inside the building, gave his heart to Christ out under the stars and the angels in Heaven looked down and rejoiced with us.

During the service, hearts were greatly moved as we looked into the faces of the children and realized that there was no place for the children to meet for Sunday school except under the trees, sometimes standing in the mud. In that service, we as a work team made a commitment to the Lord and to the church that all who could, would return next year. Our goal is to build a sanctuary three times the size of the present building. The old building will be used for children's classes and other activities.

What great things the Lord has done—and is doing today!

In Cantel, an Indian village where we have held pastors' conferences and work camps in the past, we saw the continuing fruits of the labors of so many. Once again, the building was filled. Most of the work campers were moved to the platform—and still the people came, until the church was filled and many were standing outside the doorway in the street. The youth choir and instrumental band especially blessed our hearts. We felt as if Heaven had come down and glory filled our souls.

Because of the blending of joy and sorrow in what we saw and experienced, our lives can never be the same. Even so, Lord, remind us again and again. Keep our vision clear, lest we forget.

"...Lift up your eyes, and look on the fields; for they are white already to harvest" (John 4:35 KJV).

Roma Lee

A Side Trip

February 1993

Life is a journey. There are times when the journey is difficult. Most of the time it is beautiful and exciting. Along the way, there are unusual and unexpected side trips. Such were my experiences when I attended Maya Language School in Antigua, Guatemala. Students can enroll in classes for two weeks, two months, two years, or whatever time is desired. I started by attending for two weeks on three different occasions. It was great. My next time to attend was for one month and later for two months. There were many side trips in and near Antigua. There were some weekend trips. The following experiences are excerpts from letters to my family.

Letters from Antigua, Guatemala

Dear Family,

I miss you all. You are always in my prayers. I am enjoying my study of the beautiful Spanish language. (I do admit it is difficult for a sixty-five year old woman).

This afternoon, I went to the charity hospital to help care for babies and small children. These children have been abandoned for various reasons. Parents may not be able to provide food for them or they are very ill or crippled. Some are orphans. Families know they will be cared for at the hospital. For some, this is the only home they will know. A large part of the hospital is a school. As the children grow up, they continue to live there and attend school there.

Sometimes when I go to the hospital, I help feed the little ones, put on their pajamas, and put them to bed. Today, I just held them and gave comfort. Some of the toddler-aged children have been badly burned. A tiny girl had such severe burns, her lips were turned inside out and her nose was almost burned off. A little boy, about three years old, had one side of his face burned and seared. One of his ears was missing. He was so precious and full of personality. He asked me right away how to say my name. Crying babies needed comfort. One of the babies that I held was burning with fever. Nurses give the best care they can. There are just not enough nurses.

Sunday is Valentine's Day. I have already been celebrating. I believe if there is anything to celebrate, you should start early and keep the celebration going as long as possible. If there is nothing to celebrate, think of something! I certainly hope all of you have your Valentine cards in the mail to me.

In Spanish, the words for Valentine's Day are "El dia de Amor"—the day of love. I like that! This morning, I gave my teacher a tape of Christian music. This afternoon, I went to the bakery and bought bags of Valentine cookies. I will share the cookies with my Indian friends, with everyone in the school office, and with Rosita, in whose home I live.

Almost everyday, there are various celebrations. There is music and dancing in the streets. Last week, I saw the dancing *abuelitas*, "little grandmothers." I had gone to pick up my laundry when I heard loud music. I went closer to see what was going on. There were twelve little grandmothers dancing in the street. They were all wearing long dresses, very worn-out canvas shoes, black stockings, and an old woman mask.

My first thought was, "I wonder if they get paid for this?" (I am always looking for job opportunities. Certainly, you all know I am a willing and hard worker.) I began thinking of how I might fit into this group. A few more days on these cobblestone streets and I will have very worn-out canvas shoes. I even have a pair of black stockings. With an old woman mask (maybe I don't even need a mask), I will look as good as the rest. Just when my heart was pumping with excitement, someone told me something that disqualified me. I could never be a part of the group—the little grandmothers were all men!

I have already sent you pictures of a beautiful young Indian mother, Magdalena, and her one-year-and-three-month-old daughter, Veronica. Let me tell you more about them.

I had stepped out of a photography shop. I paused to look at the photos that I just picked up. I felt a tug on my sleeve. A tiny hand was holding on tight. When I looked around, a little face smiled at me. Two little arms reached out to me. A little child on her mother's back had taken hold of my heart. It was little Veronica. Her mother Magdalena and I visited for perhaps five minutes. I asked her if she and Veronica would like to go with me for ice cream. We talked while we ate ice cream. She, her husband, and five children live in the village of San Antonio. By the time we finished our ice cream, she asked me if I would like to visit in her home. I accepted her invitation.

She asked, "Will you come tomorrow?" I would be able to go when I got out of class, but Magdalena sits on the sidewalk six days a week selling things she has made. She sells during the day and weaves more cloth at night. She assured me that her friend would sit and sell her wares for her.

As soon as I was out of class on Wednesday, Magdalena, little Veronica, and I hurried to the bus station. As we arrived at the bus station, I noticed a fast food restaurant near the bus parking lot. I asked permission to buy chicken for her family. With a bag of chicken in hand, we found a seat on the bus. I think the bus driver has no schedule. He just waits until the bus is full. Full means three persons in each seat and two persons in the aisle between the seats. We waited and waited and waited. The Indian people wait very quietly. It seemed to me there should be entertainment. I reached into my bag of precious things and took out pictures of my grandchildren. I tried to liven things up with stories. Everyone wanted to see the pictures. (Bet you all are sorry you missed that trip!)

I heard someone ask Magdalena, "Who is this woman?"

She answered, "She is my companion."

Finally the bus was full and we were on our way to San Antonio. The third person in the seat with me was a tiny, frail, very old woman. When the bus was bouncing and shaking on dirt roads, I was afraid she would fall out of the seat. I put my arm around her and held on to her. I shouldn't have worried though. There was nowhere for her to fall. The floor was already full.

San Antonio reminded me of villages in Mexico. The poverty was evident. The wind was blowing dust into my face and eyes.

When we arrived at Magdalena's home, her husband Imeldo and her four other children were there to greet us. The boys were shy, and the girls were jumping up and down clapping their hands.

We sat in a small room with bamboo walls to enjoy lunch and fellowship. There was a place on the dirt floor where Magdalena makes a fire to cook tortillas and black beans. Their table is about half the size of a card table. There are not enough chairs for all the family. The children did, as they were accustomed to doing. Veronica sat in a homemade playpen. One child sat on a small straw mat and the other children on small chairs or low stools.

After lunch, Imeldo and Magdalena asked questions about my life. They wanted to know where I lived. Did I have a family? And why was I in Antigua? No one in Antigua knows anything about me except the director at the school. I am known only by my first name. No one even knows where I live in Antigua. Now Imeldo and Magdalena want to know everything about me.

I prayed that I might have words to tell about my life, my family and why I was in Antigua. Most of all, I wanted to give testimony of my walk with the Lord.

In my Spanish class, my teacher allowed me to close the session each day by reading the booklet *¿Quieres Creer?*[1] The booklet explains God's plan of salvation and what it means to live the Christian life. After I shared my personal testimony, I read

1. Published by Stonecroft Ministries, http://www.stonecroft.org.

¿Quieres Creer? to the family. As I finished reading, other adult family members arrived. I heard Imeldo tell them my testimony and the story in the book. All the family asked for a copy of the book.

Later, we took a walk in the village. I saw the school where the children attended. I saw the shop where Imeldo worked, making jewelry. I met other beautiful village people. Both Magdalena and Imeldo insisted that I visit again the next week. They said they would cook black beans and tortillas for me.

As I was leaving, Magdalena walked with me to the bus stop. As we walked, she pointed up to a little house on the side of the mountain.

"My grandmother lives there," she said.

I told her that when I returned, I would bring fruit and banana bread and we would visit her grandmother.

Later—
Each day I looked forward to my next visit to San Antonio.

When I arrived, Magdalena had a pot of black beans cooking over the open fire. She waited for my arrival to make tortillas. She made the dough, kneaded the dough, rolled the dough, and then made the dough into little round balls. Her small hands fairly flew as she was patting the dough into perfect round tortillas. Then, it was my turn to make tortillas. I just didn't have the skill. The children were laughing in amazement that a grown woman did not know how to make tortillas. After a delicious lunch, I asked if I could take pictures of the family. Magdalena asked me if I would like to put on typical Indian dress and be in the family picture.

Eager to please and to be a part of their lives, I said, "Yes."

Magdalena is a very tiny person, perhaps weighing as much as seventy-five pounds, so I assumed there must be a large lady next door that would loan me one of her outfits.

Magdalena shooed everyone out of the room so that I could undress. Then she handed me one of her outfits. Fortunately, the women wear long straight skirts that wrap around. So, I thought maybe the skirt would do. Their blouses are cut full in body but have small necks and arm holes. I took one look at the blouse and told her it was much too small. She insisted that I must try to get it on. I had the blouse over my head and my arms about halfway in, but then I couldn't get in or out. I can tell you that when you are only halfway in an Indian blouse, you are neither in nor out!

Finally, we got me out of the blouse and I just wanted to forget the idea of me being in Indian dress—but not so with Magdalena. She clipped a thread on each sleeve that she thought would allow me to get the blouse on. But around the neck was solid handwork—beautiful flowers and fancy stitches that could not be cut. Still, she insisted I try again. This time, my arms went through but my head would not.

Magdalena was saying, *"Duro, Roma Lee, mas duro!"* I told her that my head was too fat. But she kept saying, "Duro, mas duro." (Duro means hard.) I told her that I would have no hair left on my head. I doubt there has ever been so much laughter within those walls. The Lord being my merciful helper, I finally got the blouse on.

Next, was a trip to grandmother's house. As we climbed the mountain, the view was beautiful. Grandmother was sitting at her loom weaving cloth. Perhaps, it was some of her crafts that Magdalena sells. Grandmother was sweet, gracious and grateful for the gift of food. Every day brings a new adventure and learning experience.

Every day, I think of my wonderful family at home. I am so blessed.

My love to each of you,
Mom

Top: The work campers drove from Tennessee to Guatemala in this bus towing a truck.

Bottom: Magdalena making tortillas for lunch in a house with bamboo walls.

Top: Roma Lee visiting with an Indian mother on the streets of Antigua.
Bottom: Roma Lee with three generations of Indian women.

CHAPTER 7

Nicaragua

Roma Lee took work camps to Costa Rica for many years and worked with the Lopezes. Amina Lopez had a brother, Nour Sirker, who was a doctor in Nicaragua.

"Roma Lee, you have done so much for the people of Costa Rica, but my brother is in Nicaragua. The people there are more needy. Please go and help them," requested Amina.

Roma Lee needed no other encouragement. She and one other woman went to Nicaragua to meet with Nour and Carolyn Sirker to determine the pressing needs in that country. God opened the door to a new arena of ministry and she walked through the door. When Roma Lee began her ministry in Nicaragua at the end of the civil war, the Sandinistas were still very much a threat.

Roma Lee recalled, "You had to be very careful of anything you said, even in church. Someone might be in the church and hear something they thought was against the Sandinistas. People could be arrested right in church. The printed propaganda for the group was beautiful. It was full color and stated how good the government was with them in power. You could look out the door of the church and see that the situation of the people was not good."

In Her Own Words

November 1992 Newsletter, "From My Heart to You."

Managua, Nicaragua, September 1992...It was not yet midmorning, but already it was hot and humid. Our clothes felt damp and clingy on our bodies. But how can one complain about the heat when you have witnessed the devastation of a land and people. These are people who have been lashed by the natural disasters of volcano eruptions, earthquakes, and tidal waves. Even worse than natural disasters were the years of bondage and suffering from national leadership and then ten years of civil war.

The building team was already working on an additional room for the clinic in Managua. Two medical teams had left for their clinic work sites. The third medical team was still waiting for the van that would take them to the village of Tipitapa. In the village, there would be at least 250 persons waiting to receive medical aid. They would be waiting in the building, in the yard, and in the street. It wasn't hard to imagine what needs might be waiting for the workers. Pictures of patients, already seen in the past few days, were clearly in our minds. One woman's leg was infected from the knee down. The infection had eaten away all the skin leaving only open flesh consumed with infection. When asked how long her leg had been infected, she replied, "Three years." There was a child prostitute only fourteen years of age. A man using a butcher knife had slashed her face, limbs, and body.

The sick, the lame, the blind came. They waited for hours in the sun and heat. Medical teams worked hour after hour, and at the close of the day, many still had to be turned away. All of these things were remembered as the third medical team waited for the van to take them to Tipitapa. They wondered why the van driver did not hurry to get them. (Soon the group would know the reason for the delay; everything had to happen in perfect timing with God's plans. Soon they would know that the most important event of the day would happen before they reached Tipitapa.)

At last, the van arrived and ten people crowded into the small van. There was one stop to make on the way to the village clinic—the pharmacy. Each day a new supply of medicine and vitamins had to be purchased. The van was parked a short distance from the pharmacy. The doctors left to purchase supplies. It only took a few minutes for the group to decide it was much too hot to stay in the van. It would be better to walk to the pharmacy.

As they walked, they saw a man approaching them. When he came near, he reached out and touched one of the women. He spoke, but she did not understand his words. There was something different about his eyes, as if something was wrong. His head was drawn to one side, as though it wasn't centered with his body. The decision now was, "Shall we walk faster (caution is our rule for the street) or shall we stop and see what he needs?"

The man spoke again. His words were, "I want to know Jesus. Can you tell me about Jesus? I have no hope, no one cares about me, and no one loves me. I have tried drugs and drink. I have tried to kill myself. I tried to hang myself, but it didn't work. I have cut my arms and I didn't die." (He held out his arms showing where slashes had been made. The open wounds had now become infected.)

He continued speaking, "I decided that this would be the day that I would find a way to kill myself because I have no hope." The man dropped to his knees and began to weep.

One person in the group shared the beautiful story of Jesus and His love and then led the man in a prayer for forgiveness and acceptance of Jesus. When the man rose from his knees, all those present witnessed the transformation. His face was radiant, his eyes clear, and his head erect. One of the nurses cleansed, medicated, and bound up the wounds on his arms. He was given a Bible, which he accepted with joy and promised to read it every day.

Someone then asked the question, "How did you know to come to us?"

His answer was, "When I saw you coming down the street, I saw a light around you. I walked to the light. I thought maybe you could tell me about Jesus."

How silently, how silently, the wondrous gift is given.
So God imparts to human hearts, the blessings of His heaven.
No ear may hear His coming, but in this world of sin,
Where meek souls will receive Him still,
The dear Christ enters in. (Philip Brooks)

O Come Let Us Adore Him!

Roma Lee

Managua, Nicaragua
Holiday Greetings 1995 (Excerpt)

I must find the child. My heart cried out for her. I would know her when I saw her. She would be small, about nine years old. Her hair would be dirty and matted. Her dress would be ragged. Her feet would be bare. I would reach out to her, and she would run into my arms. My eyes and heart searched for the child.

Sometimes she could be found in the parking area near a market. She, like many children in Latin America, works on the streets and in parking areas asking to guard cars for a few cents.

Recently when missionaries Dr. Nour and Carolyn Sirker were teaching a Bible class for children, Carolyn noticed that one child did not come inside. She remained outside sitting on a step behind the church. When invited to come inside, she answered, "I can't because I have no shoes." After being assured that she was welcome, she joined the other children. She quietly went away after class. No one knew where she lived. The next week, she came to Bible class again.

In the next few days, the Sirkers saw her several times near the market—the dirty barefoot child—not begging for a handout but asking to guard cars.

When I heard about the child, I knew I must find her. Several times in the next two days, Carolyn and I looked for her. We asked workers in the area if they had seen the little girl with no shoes guarding cars. No one had seen her or knew who she was. We decided to check a wider area. We spoke with all the children who were helping their mothers sell fruits and vegetables. In answer to our questions, everyone shook their heads.

A girl lying crumpled in a wheelbarrow raised her head to say, "No," that she did not know the person we were looking for. But as we walked away, she called us back.

She said, "You mean The Cat. I'll show you where she lives."

When we realized our young guide was taking us into an unsafe area, we removed our cheap jewelry (watch and earrings) and put them in our pockets. Then our guide, looking out for our safety said, "Wait here. I'll go find her."

Soon both girls came hurrying back to us. There she was. The beautiful child with matted hair, no shoes, and a smile to melt my heart. The little brown arms were reaching out to me. Her name is Janete. The children call her, "The Cat," because her eyes are a light greenish brown. She lives with her grandmother. There is no mother or father in the home. There are nine people living in the small house.

Janete is nine years old and has never been to school. She has not been to school because there is no money for clothes, books, or fees. I asked her if she would like to go to school. With excitement, she answered, "Si, si!" I promised her that I would be her madrina (godmother), that she could go to school, and that she would have clothes and shoes.

We visited the grandmother to be sure that she approved of Janete's going to school. The smile on her face showed the gratitude in her heart.

In January, when I return to Nicaragua, one suitcase will contain ribbons, bows, shoes, dresses, and maybe even a doll for a special little girl. In February (starting the new school year), Janete will walk proudly down the street in a new school uniform and new school shoes with a bag of books to attend first grade in a Christian school.

You are treasured in my heart, and I think of you always with love.

Roma Lee

Managua, Nicaragua
February 1996

It was February 19, 1996, a hot, humid day in Managua. Perspiration rolled down our faces, but no one's spirit was dampened. Excitement was high. There were perhaps 150 children outside the gate by 8:30 a.m. Mothers with babies or small children in their arms pressed close to the gate.

It was opening day and "Inaugracion" ceremonies for Escuela Christiana Emilia de Sirker. There were moist eyes as we watched children in crisp white shirts and blouses, navy pants and skirts, marched into the courtyard for opening ceremonies. For many children, some as old as eleven, this would be their first time to attend school.

Families in barrio Santa Rosa, Managua, are extremely poor. Seldom can they afford to send all their children to school. For some, they are unable to send even one child.

On February 19, we saw visible fruits of many prayers, labors, and gifts. Years ago, Emilia Sirker dreamed of and prayed for a Christian school in Santa Rosa. Four groups of North Americans worked in the construction of the school; others gave gifts of money for building materials. Yet even this was not enough to make the dream a reality. The children must have sponsors in order to attend the school. As in many schools, the children must have uniforms, books, and other school supplies, and teachers must have a small salary. Caring hearts responded to this need also. And that is why there is a new light in Santa Rosa, the light of a Christian school in a community where there is little Christian witness. A children's Bible club will be held each week in the school. There will be other Christian activities, as well.

The building is truly beautiful, painted in bright Latin colors. Deep-red tile floors, a mural on one wall in each classroom, chalkboards, and bulletin boards make it complete. But the beauty of the school in no way compares to the beauty in the faces of the children.

There were many thoughts of praise and prayer flooding my mind and heart as inaugracion ceremonies began. First, I was amazed to see the children standing with such order and respect for more than an hour in the hot sun. Looking at the children,

I felt such gratitude to be part of all that was happening on this day. I rejoiced even more to realize the potential in the lives of the children to become Christian leaders in homes, communities, and government. This day could be the beginning of hope in hearts where there is little hope.

I wish you could know the children that I have come to love so much. They are all special, all needy, sometimes hungry, and always melt your heart. Let me introduce you to some of them.

Julio and Julia are brother and sister. Both are loving, well-mannered, and helpful. They live with other family members in a small house with no conveniences such as water, bathroom, or even a kitchen. Their food is cooked on an open fire in the yard. Since there are several younger children in the family, I have observed how well Julio and Julia care for the younger ones—holding them, washing faces, dressing them, or giving comfort to a crying child. Both Julio and Julia want to study. They want to learn. Last year, their mother enrolled them in public school. The school kept demanding money, but they had no money to pay. This meant they could not receive grades, a promotion, or continue in school. Julio and Julia are now sponsored by a group of children in Kansas. They are attending the Christian school in Santa Rosa.

Ivan lives in a small, very dark house in an alley. When you step inside the house, your eyes have to adjust to the darkness. There are no windows in the house, except for an opening near the open fire, over which his mother cooks tortillas. Ivan is small and frail. He never seemed to feel well. He has not been checked by a doctor or received medication. He is attending the new school. The first time I saw Ivan smile was when I gave him a bright new book bag from his sponsor.

Of all the precious children I have met in Nicaragua, I think my heart has been touched most by Juan Carlos, the little boy that no one wants. His mother did not want him, so when he was two months old, she gave him to her sister, who did not really want him either. The aunt, whom Juan Carlos calls "Mother," has ten children of her own. She has tried to give him to someone else. She tells him, "You are a bad boy. You are not good. I don't want you. Get out of my house." So he wanders the streets until late at night.

One night recently, he witnessed a murder on the street. He knew how many times the man was shot, described every detail, and said, "There was blood all over the street." The newspaper carried the story exactly as Juan Carlos had described it.

He often stays with the Sirkers (missionaries) on weekends, so he gets to know the North American work groups well. His eyes sparkle when he says, "The North Americans love me!" He looks forward to eating with us. He especially loves to go with us to the Pizza Hut. As eight large pizzas were being served at our long table, he looked up and asked, "Will there be food for my family or should I save some of mine?"

God bless each of you who have either directly or indirectly touched the lives of children in Nicaragua. You are making a difference.

I was just thinking it takes more than a village to raise a child. It takes a world!

From my heart to yours, I send a world of thanks and love!
Roma Lee

Top: Carolyn Sirker (left) and Roma Lee (right)
Bottom Left: The entry to the Escuela Christina Emilia de Sirker school in Managua, Nicaragua.
Bottom Right: Janete and Roma Lee

CHAPTER 8

Ecuador

Roma Lee went to Ecuador long before there was a work of the Church of God. As with all countries, she loved the work of the church and loved the people.

In 1997, Ecuador suffered the effects of El Niño. The devastation ranged from flooding to drought, which led to people starving.

One night in her home in Middletown, Ohio, Roma Lee had a dream.

"I was back in Meridiano and there was no food. The landslides had washed the crops away. I dreamed that the people were crying for food and dying. In my dream, I kept saying, 'I have to go. I have to get there and help them.' I could never see who was in the dream, but there was a person who said, 'You can't go.'" related Roma Lee.

"When I woke up, I had actually been crying and there were tears on my pillow. I told Lynette [her daughter] that I had to get money quickly and take it to buy food for the people. I knew that God spoke to David of old in a dream. I knew the dream was from God."

Roma Lee understood the urgency of her mandate from the Lord. She raised $12,000 in a matter of a few days. She took the money to Ecuador to purchase food. When she arrived in Ecuador, she met two men, one of whom was a pastor, who had traveled for two days down the mountain from Meridiano. They traveled to Quito not knowing what they could do to help solve the dire situation in their village. They knew that the people were starving. The people were digging up roots to try to survive. The children cried because the roots hurt their stomachs after they ate them.

While in Meridiano, the pastor had prayed, "Does anyone care that we have no food? God, do you care that we have no food?"

Upon finding out that there was food for his village, the pastor was so thrilled that he didn't let the challenge of getting the food up the mountainside hinder his joy. The churches in Quito planned a service of praise for the food, but they delayed the service so the two men could go back up the mountain to relay the message of hope to the villagers.

Using trucks as far as the roads were built and then putting the food on horseback the remainder of the route to the village solved the challenge of food distribution.

In 2009, when Roma Lee coordinated the food distribution in Ecuador for the last time, she took $85,470. She not only took cash in money belts but also sewed it into the pockets of her jeans. She shared the responsibility with other work campers. She personally has carried up to $25,000 on her person. God has protected her time and time again as she carried money needed for missions projects.

With no formal training in fundraising, Roma Lee shared, "I know that God does not just drop money on your doorstep. As with all of missions, personal relationships are the key in raising money and soliciting prayer support. I knew people's joys and sorrows. When someone personally sacrifices to send money, I write a personal note of appreciation."

The funds for the food ministry came from many sources, one of which was an older couple, David and Goldie Parker, a retired pastor and his wife in Kansas. They sent all the profits from yard sales to Roma Lee for the Food for Ecuador fund.

As the couple increasingly grew older, Goldie would say to Roma Lee, "I think this will be our last sale. We just aren't able to physically have the sales any more."

Soon, Roma Lee would get another check from the couple from yet another yard sale. In time, Goldie had to place her husband into the nursing home. Roma Lee continued to minister to her by calling her and sending her devotional books for comfort. Since Roma Lee had placed her husband into the nursing home, she was able to minister from the heart out of her personal experience.

Roma Lee shared, "It is a matter of doing God's work, whatever that is." Whether it is in local missions, foreign missions, sending devotional books, making phone calls, or praying for those with special needs. Roma Lee continues to listen to God's leading.

In Her Own Words

It's Christmas Time, 1991

Hearts always go home for Christmas—either in reality or memory.

Someone has said, "Home is where the heart is." This Christmas, my heart is in many places. My heart is in the deserts, mountains, jungles, villages, cities, and everywhere I have learned to love people.

I have come to realize that home is the center of God's will. And that is where we find real peace, hope, joy and love. It is in this place, I most desire to be.

As I reflect back on the events of 1991, I wonder, "Did it all happen in one year?" There has been so much joy, and blessings, but there have also been difficulties and pain. Through it all, I have learned how sure and faithful is God's love and that of family and friends.

My heart has been at home in many places as we have worked, prayed, and served together in Mexico, Guatemala, Costa Rica, Peru, and Ecuador.

There are stories and experiences from each place that I would like to share with you, but since this is not possible, I will share one highlight experience.

We were with the church in Quito, Ecuador, for their Missions Sunday. This is a congregation of new believers—a mission church. There was special music, drama and a challenging message from the pastor. Faith promise commitment cards were used. There was so much excitement in the hearts of these new Christians for giving and going with the gospel. What an inspiration and challenge to us who have so much more in resources to go and do likewise.

I recently received a special blessing from work campers. This summer, I moved again. The house needed some work upstairs and the basement was totally unfinished. Then came a group of "work campers" to do the work. We had a weekend mini-work camp. Then once again when I was working in Peru, work campers returned to complete my house. I returned from Peru to a finished house. I now can say that I live in a house that love built. *Thank you, work campers!*

As you know, I have had health problems this year. I was diagnosed as having lupus. This is a disease that is usually found in younger women (my body even thought I was younger).

There is much weakness and pain associated with the illness. There is no cure and not much treatment. Many prayers have been said in my behalf. I have had a definite touch of healing from the Lord. I am still going, still praising, still trusting and expecting total complete healing.

How can I say thanks to you who so faithfully continue to be a part of the work of missions? You have gone in His Name and the results can be seen in the construction of buildings, medicine given from loving hands, and God's Word prayerfully given to hundreds. You have made a difference in many lives—you have made a difference in my life.

My heart is with you this Christmas and I wish for you peace, hope, joy and...

Especially Love,
Roma Lee

July 1995

Tears glistened in her eyes as she asked us to pray for her. Maria is a new Christian. Only one week ago, she made a commitment of her life to Jesus Christ. She is a beautiful young woman in her early twenties. She has four beautiful children. She gives her children much attention and affection. There is a part of Maria's life that is not beautiful, but very difficult and painful. Maria lives in Zabala, a community on the outskirts of Quito.

I remember the first time that I saw Zabala. I stood on the side of a mountain and looked down on the valley. There were hundreds of people living there. In every direction, small houses were under construction. It was a poor but growing community. I could see children playing in the dusty roads and women carrying buckets of water as they hurried home to prepare the evening meal. The wind was blowing and dust was blowing in the wind. Compared to the lush beauty of the surrounding green mountains, Zabala looked like a desert.

I was told that there was no church in the valley of Zabala.

"No church?" I asked.

"No church of any kind or denomination," was the reply.

I watched as evening dusk and darkness settled over Zabala. I could imagine Jesus looking over the valley and weeping for "such as sit in darkness and in the shadow of death, being bound in affliction…" (Psalm 107:10a KJV).

After I returned home, I spoke at a weekend retreat concerning the need for a church in Zabala.

A single mother with two children said, "I want to give my savings to buy the land for the church building." Jesus must have smiled to see such dedication.

The next year, we returned to Zabala with workers to begin construction of the church. I thank God for those who gave funds for building materials and for those who labored in the "valley of dust." The midday sun is hot in Zabala. The little tornados (whirlwinds) often filled eyes and faces with dirt. One time, the wind took down the newly laid block wall. Water was carried in buckets to where the cement was mixed on the ground. Then buckets and wheelbarrows of cement were taken to the men laying block. In the afternoon, some of the work campers held Bible school for the children. We started with sixty-five children but grew to two hundred twenty. Also, fifteen mothers attended because they loved to hear the Bible stories and songs.

On the last day of the work camp, tearful mothers and children came to say good-bye. They thanked everyone for coming to Zabala. Two questions were asked: "When will you come again?" and "When will we have a church?"

The following year, workers did return. At the end of the work camp, there was a service of dedication and praise. Some made decisions for Christ.

We returned again to Zabala to visit in homes, to pray, to give and receive hugs and kisses, and to worship with those we love so dearly. What a sweet, sweet sound as we joined together to sing in Spanish and English. "Gozo hay en Jesus," "There is joy in the Lord."[1]

Maria lives just across the road in front of the church. She lives in one small room with her four children. She has two small beds and a stove. Her children have the same father, but their father is married and has other children. There is no possibility that he will ever care for Maria or her children. Maria, in tears, asked that we pray for her.

She said, "I am a Christian now, and I want to live a different life. I want a Christian home for my children. Pray for me."

As our group went aside to pray with Maria, there was a special presence in our midst. He came as softly as a dove descending. He gave the warmth of fire in our hearts, and He smiled because "the people that walked in darkness have seen a great light; they that dwell in the land of the shadow of death, upon them hath the light shined" (Isaiah 9:2 KJV).

Money was left with the missionaries to pay for enrolling Maria in a vocational school, pay for childcare while she attends classes, and help provide food for the children.

My Prayer:
Lord, I thank you for all those who have helped to bring life and hope to others. For all who have given to make life better for

1. "There Is Joy in the Lord." Lyrics by Barney Warren.

Maria, and others like her. For all who have helped to feed and clothe the "least of these." For the suitcases filled with treats that bring smiles to dirty, little faces.

And Lord, I thank you for allowing me to go, to be your hands extended. My heart is humbled in gratitude and love to you and to all those who have helped to send me. Bless them each one, according to your abundant love and grace. Amen.

Roma Lee

P.S. In case you wonder where I have been and why I haven't answered my phone much lately, the reason is because for eleven months of this year, I will have been in one and often two foreign countries each month. My life is busy and blessed. You are part of the blessings. Thanks!

April 26, 1999

As the plane soars into the heavens, I look through the window to see the beautiful city of Quito below. It is always hard to leave people you love, but especially hard today. The people here are experiencing hardships and hunger greater than I have seen in this country before. They are having great difficulties both with the political and economic situation.

Without warning, all banks in Ecuador closed for one week. When banks reopened, the president ordered that all assets over $500.00 in all accounts be frozen for one year. This left businesses without funds for operation. They did not have funds for supplies or salaries. Businesses large and small began to close. More businesses close daily. Each day hundreds more find themselves without employment and no way to earn money for daily bread. During the time I have been in Quito, five more banks closed. I see the needs at their worst, because I work with the very poor.

Some of the greatest needs are in the rural community of Meridiano. This small community is about four hours (or more) up the mountain. In the best of times, these people have little food. They sawed the trees and built small houses. They have no transportation except for those who own a horse. With horse and plow, they farm small plots of land on the mountainside. Usually, they raise tangerines and corn that they eat—and hope to have some to sell so they can buy other food supplies. In the past, a bus took food supplies to Meridiano. Basic foods such as beans, rice, flour and oil and other supplies such as matches and soap were sold to two small storeowners. More recently, the people have not had corn or tangerines to eat or sell and no money to buy food supplies. The bus no longer takes the supplies there. For many weeks, the people have had no food except to go into the woods every morning to dig for any kind of roots that they might be able to eat.

Two pastors from Meridiano arrived in Quito before my arrival. They were hoping to find work there. One pastor said that recently while sitting at his table with only roots for his family to eat, he asked God, "Does anyone care that we have no food. God, do you care that we have no food?"

When he learned that soon we would be sending a truck with food to Meridiano, he decided to make the long journey back up the mountain to share the good news. After telling the good news, this pastor and two others walked for many hours, traveling three days to return to Quito for a unity praise service on Sunday evening.

Being a part of buying and packing food for Meridiano was one of the greatest blessings I have experienced. For each family, we bought forty-four pounds of flour, five gallons of oil, rice, beans, pasta, sugar, chicken and beef bouillon, cocoa mix, vitamin drink mix, popcorn, salt, matches, and soap.

Food was provided for six churches and two preaching points. In each of these places, extra food and supplies were given so the churches could share with others in their community. The gratitude of the people was more than words can describe. One person said, "To give us oil is like giving us gold!"

Many of you will remember Victoria, the little short woman with a big smile and an even bigger heart. She lives in a tiny hut on the side of a mountain. She teaches a Bible class for children in her yard. She has fifty children in her class, and they are still growing. Most of these children do not have fathers in the home. They do not have mothers who attend church, but since they are some of the most needy in the city, we provided the same amount of food for each family as the others received.

Sunday evening, Victoria brought about thirty-five of her children, along with several mothers, to the praise service. At the close of the service, three of the mothers committed their lives to Christ.

I could tell you so much more, but this gives you a glimpse of needs and how God is working.

Roma Lee

1999: Mission Update and Notes of Praise!!

From April through August, I have been working in South America. I have been twice to Ecuador and five times to Peru during this five-month period.

In April, we took funds to Ecuador to purchase food. Ecuador is still in an economic depression. Twice a year, we take funds to help in this crisis. We buy staples such as rice, beans, pasta, oatmeal, flour, sugar, oil, milk, tuna, etc.

The people say, "We have learned to stretch the food. Still it is not enough."

The word from Ecuador is, "Our people are hungry."

I will be going back to Ecuador the first week of October. As in the past, we need at least $15,000 for food. Actually, we need more than this amount. The churches are growing. We now have more families who need our help.

Blessings,
Roma Lee

September, 2001 *(Excerpts)*

"Feed My Lambs—Feed My Sheep"

I have just been thinking about a conversation between Jesus and Simon Peter.

Jesus said to Peter, "Do you truly love me?"

"Yes, Lord," he said, "You know that I love you."

Jesus said, "Take care of my sheep."

Again Jesus said, "Do you truly love me?"

He answered, "Yes, Lord, you know all things, you know that I love you."

Jesus said, "Feed my sheep" (John 21:16–17).

I think the conversation was not just between Peter and Jesus. I keep hearing Him whisper that question to me.

Of course, my quick response is, "Yes, Lord, you know that I love you."

His reply to me, "Feed my lambs; feed my sheep."

It is more than just words that move my heart. I can see faces of people I know and love, faces of those who know what it is to be hungry. Parents who hear their children cry for bread when there is no bread. Fathers who ask the question, "Lord, do you care that my children are hungry? Does anyone care that my family is hungry?"

Jesus hears and cares. Then He does a marvelous but risky thing. He turns the responsibility for the answer over to us who say we love Him. How else can we prove our love for Him but to care for His lambs and sheep?

Did He not say, "I tell you the truth, whatever you did not do for one of the least of these, you did not do for me" (Matthew 25:45).

Some of you know that since early in 1999, the country of Ecuador has been in major economic depression. Some of the children have been so malnourished that their black hair turned an orange-red and came out.

People of the rural mountain community of Meridiano survived for weeks and weeks with only roots to eat. Each day they went into the woods to dig for any kind of roots—even roots that they didn't know could be eaten. These people have experienced some of the worst physical suffering.

Many of you have given to the Food for Ecuador Fund. You have made a difference for so many. I have seen the difference. I go every six months, along with others, to deliver the funds. We work with missionaries and national leaders to buy and distribute the food. Those who receive the food share their food with others in their communities.

Even in the midst of the worst of times, the churches continue to experience revival and growth. We continue to pray that soon there will be a change in the economic situation. For now, there is still need to give help. Because of the extra food, their health has improved. Most of the children have plump cheeks and smiles. We see only a few children who still have a red cast on their hair.

We continue to buy the same amount of staple foods per family. Because of the increase in the number of families, the amount of food and funds must also increase. We hope that this supplement, with whatever they can do for themselves, will sustain them for six months each time. In April, we took $23,118.00. Every cent was needed. We will go again in October. We are asking God to provide $25,000. Is anything too hard for God?

Blessings, love, and gratitude to you from all who receive from you generous heart and hands.

Little brown child
Far over the sea
Reaching your thin
Little arms out to me.

Pain, fear and famine
Have long been your part.
Can I refuse you
A place in my heart?

Grief stricken mother
Your eyes on my face
What if some day
I should stand in your place?

Watching my baby
Lie dying for bread,
While millions of others
Are cherished and fed.

I pray, Lord Jesus
Look down from above,
Grant me the tenderness,
Grant me thy love.

Cast out all fetters
Of color and creed,
Help me see only
Thy children in need.[2]

As always, from my heart to yours.

Love and appreciation,
Roma Lee

Newsletter circa 2000–2001 *(Excerpts)*

$30,929.00 Given for Ecuador Food Fund
Hundreds of people received food. What a blessing to be in Ecuador when a great multitude is fed!

I thought, "It's a Miracle!" I also thought of you who were a part of the miracle.

2. Author unknown.

It was a heart-touching experience to see those who received food giving to others in need. They are not told to do this. It is their way of giving back to the Lord.

A new problem in Ecuador is that 20% of the population has left the country to seek work in other countries (most seem to be going to Spain). Many parents are leaving children with grandparents or other relatives. These are desperate people trying to survive. But it means more children in need of food.

You will note that $5,481.00 will be used to provide extra food for Christmas. Families who would have nothing special for Christmas will now have a special Christmas dinner. They will receive chickens, cake, extra rice, and more.

Jesus spoke about what you have done. He said, "Come, you who are blessed by my Father; take your inheritance, the kingdom prepared for you since the creation of the world. For I was hungry and you gave me something to eat" (Matthew 25:34–35).

Thank you for caring. Thank you for giving.

Enjoy your Christmas dinner. May your heart and home be filled with....

Blessing and Love,
Roma Lee

P.S. For your information, each family received: flour, sugar, rice, red beans, white beans, lentils, oatmeal, quinoa (seeds of the plant are cooked in a way similar to cooking rice), popcorn, maicena (corn flour), coffee, cocoa, powdered milk, butter, oil, tuna, bullion cubes, baking powder, pastas, Jell-O, pinol (powder made from corn to mix with water for a drink), matches, bath soap, dish detergent, shampoo, and toothpaste.

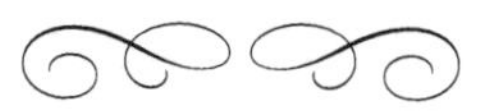

The Lord Has Enlarged Our Territory, 2002

Many of us have prayed the prayer of Jabez. "Jabez cried out to the God of Israel, 'Oh, that you would bless me and *enlarge my territory*! Let your hand be with me and keep me from harm so that I will be free from pain.' And God granted his request" (1 Chronicles 4:10, italics added).

Since 1999, we have worked together to feed hundreds in Ecuador. Twice a year, we take money to buy a six-month supply of food staples. This, along with what they do for themselves, has been lifesaving. We have seen them go from extreme malnutrition and illness to health. Without the help from Christians in the U.S., the people would suffer greatly—especially the children.

I am always thrilled and blessed to see those who receive food share so freely with others. They give thanks for the food. (Sometimes praying for an hour just thanking God.) Then they fill large sacks, which they carry on their backs. It is a beautiful sight to see them walking the dusty roads or climbing the mountain trails to share the food with others in need. Just as God blessed Jabez, He has blessed their giving. He has enlarged their territory. The churches have grown—in most places, they overflow their buildings.

The latest group to become a part of this ministry is the Cayambe Indians. There are twenty thousand Cayambes living in forty-seven communities. They are very poor. Many of the men work on rose plantations. They work seven days a week, ten hours a day for $150.00 a month. There are only three evangelical churches among them.

In November, I went with missionaries [Lamberts and Snyders] to visit a small group of Cayambes. We delivered food and met with them for their first church service. Forty-seven attended the service. We sat in a church made from poles and plastic.

One of the Cayambe men said, "This is the first time the feet of evangelicals have walked upon this land. This is the first service to praise the Lord, but we will still be here working and praising Him when He comes back for us."

As our territory is enlarged, more money is necessary to meet the need. In November, $34,202.00 was spent for the food ministry. In April, we will need $35,000. Once again, we need a miracle of love and giving. Thanks to all of you who have given in the past to help relieve the pain and hunger.

I pray the Lord to bless you. May He continue to enlarge your territory, keep you from harm and free from pain. My love and prayers surround you always.

Roma Lee

Holiday Greetings, 2005

Even now, you are probably making plans for celebrating the seasons of Thanksgiving and Christmas. Looking back and looking forward, let us give thanks.

This has been a busy and blessed year. Teams of dedicated work campers have given their time, talents, strength and money to serve the Lord in South America. Thanks to all who have gone, and to all who have been the back-up force here at home.

What did our combined efforts do?

In Peru, working with Ken Biron, a conference was held for teachers and leaders. More than 300 children attended Bible school. Building teams worked on construction. Many families received huge boxes of food. Hundreds of crafts and school supplies were given. Each girl received a beautiful doll. Each boy received a soccer ball. Families received clothing. The Breiel [Breiel Boulevard Church of God, Middletown, Ohio] choir presented a beautiful concert in Spanish. In almost every service, there were some who received the Lord. We, who traveled so far, received rewards beyond measure. In services and in homes, we knew we were standing on holy ground. Each day, we were touched (and hugged) by more than two hundred angels—the children in the school. The warmth of His Spirit and their love, we hold in our hearts forever.

In Ecuador, working with Jon and Karen Lambert is always a blessing. For many years, work campers have been going to help build churches and housing for pastors. Several years ago, we added a new ministry. After an economic and political collapse, along with a severe weather change, the country was devastated. People were hungry. The children were extremely malnourished and ill. We began the feeding program. Twice each year, food staples are bought to supplement their meager diet. I could write pages of stories to tell you how this program and your gifts help hundreds who hunger. For now, I will share only one story of a group that receives help through this program.

It is not easy to visit the community of Bela Vista. You must travel a few hours by bus. Part of the journey is over extremely rough roads. Then you come to a river. You must cross the river by walking on a swinging bridge. Then you walk, perhaps a half mile, up a trail to visit a group of new Christians. The men work on banana plantations for very little wages. In Bela Vista, no one had heard the name of Jesus in more than forty years. Imagine their suffering in poverty, sickness and death—and they didn't even know His Name!

A man from Bela Vista went to Quito looking for work. He heard Delia Rodriguez tell the story of Jesus. With joy, he received the Lord. He asked Delia to visit Bela Vista and tell the story to his people.

Among those who heard and accepted the message was Gloria, a paraplegic. Gloria was eager to tell the story, so she would struggle to get on top of a small table, open the window, and teach the children who would gather outside her window.

Delia and the Lamberts continue to visit those living in Bela Vista. The Lamberts took a wheelchair to Gloria. Now she can cross the road to the little building where she teaches the children and adults. How beautiful it is to see them gather for worship and hear their songs of praise.

Along with other team members, I will leave for Ecuador on November tenth. A special thanks to all who have given to the food program. My love and gratitude to all who have given to send me to the mission field.

I will be having surgery to replace both knees on Tuesday, November 29. I will appreciate your prayers.

Wishing You Blessed and Happy Holidays,
Roma Lee

November, 2006

"A Savior Is Born. He is Christ the Lord."
Many events have touched my life in the past few weeks. A major and unexpected change came with Frank's death on November

seventh. After twenty-five years of illness, he is free at last! Thank you for your prayers, calls, flowers, plants memorial gifts and so many expressions of love.

I was supposed to leave for Ecuador on November eighth. Even though I was unable to go, the group went; the money was sent; food was bought and delivered. The group had a wonderful experience. The grand total given for November food ministry was $44,719.89. To all who gave, thank you and God bless you.

On Thanksgiving Day, I left for Ecuador. My bags were loaded with gifts for children and the missionaries. Every day and night meant new blessings. A highlight experience for me, along with the missionaries, was wrapping all the Christmas gifts for the sponsored children. We played Christmas tapes and wrapped and wrapped gifts. By the time we finished, I felt like Christmas day had dawned.

The churches are so alive with the presence of the Lord. Even with the rain every day, the people came, willing to walk through mud and darkness. The churches were filled.

This was my first time to visit the new congregation in Ofelia. They worship in a storefront building. When you enter, you know you are in the presence of the Lord. Pastor Milton Vidal started this church in 2005. He began working with ex-convicts and their families. Pastor Milton is also an ex-convict. He grew up in poverty, having never known anything about God or His Word. He was always seeking something to fill the void in his life. He left his rural life and home in southern Ecuador when he was seventeen. He arrived in Quito with no money and no job. He began to rob and steal to survive. He was also smoking, drinking, and using drugs. He was often in and out of jail. In jail, he met other young men like himself. They formed a gang and called themselves *Banda de Terror* (Terror Gang). Once out of jail, they would get high on drugs, rob, and kill. Eventually, he was arrested and convicted of murder by eleven judges. He continued to use drugs in prison. Then he began dealing in drugs. (You can do this in Ecuador prisons). He sank lower and lower. He hated what he had become but could see no way out. Finally, he cried out, "Help me, God. If you are real, help me."

Three months later, a young woman with an evangelical group came to visit the inmates. (The young woman, Lily, would later become Milton's wife). She told Milton about God and His great love. She told him about Jesus, about forgiveness and salvation. Milton wanted to believe but felt that his sins were so great that God could not forgive him. That night, Milton could not sleep. He cried out to the Lord. He fell to his knees offering himself to God. Salvation came. Milton's life was completely changed. Later, he became pastor of the prison church. He preached, prayed, and baptized new converts.

After seven years in prison, Milton pled his case before the eleven judges that had convicted him. One judge sarcastically asked Milton how many years his "good works" should remove from his sentence.

Milton responded, "I am already free, whether in here or out there." The judges saw the change in his life. He was released from prison sixteen years early.

Milton and Lily were married. Their home became a place of Bible study and prayer. Today, they continue ministering to those released from prison, the people on the street, the very poor, and others held captive by sin.

Everyone has a story, a story of God's love and redemption. One young man told us he has the responsibility to care for his daughter and his mother. Recently, when he had a week with no sales, he had no money for food. He went to the church on his way home. The food had been delivered for all the families. He left with large boxes of food. When he arrived home, his mother saw the food and began to weep tears of joy. She said, "Now, we will eat tonight!"

The gifts of food come from many hearts and hands. Thank you again for giving to the Lord. Jesus said, "Whatever you did for one of the least of these, you did it for me" (Matthew 25:45).

Happy Birthday, Jesus!

Wishing You a World of Love,
Roma Lee

June, 2007

Jesus Feeds More Than Five Thousand

"Jesus withdrew from town to a solitary place. Hearing this, the crowds followed him. When Jesus saw the large crowd he had compassion on them and healed their sick. As evening approached, the people were hungry. The disciples wanted to send them away, but Jesus told the disciples to feed them.

'We have here only five loaves of bread and two fish,' they answered.

'Bring them here to me,' He said. And He directed the people to sit down on the grass. Taking the five loaves and the two fish and looking up to heaven, He gave thanks and broke the loaves. Then he gave them to the disciples, and the disciples gave them to the people. They all ate and were satisfied, and the disciples picked up twelve basketfuls of broken pieces that were left over. The number of those who ate was about five thousand men, besides women and children" (Matthew 14:13–21).

I am sure those who were present for the miracle that day will never quit talking about it. Even today, we picture in our minds what it would have been like to be there. Children in

Sunday school classes pretend to help pass the bread and fish to the people. Everyone wants to be part of a miracle.

There is a special miracle that many of you are part of. It is the miracle of feeding the multitudes in Ecuador. This is the eighth year of the feeding program. The food is distributed in the spring and again in the fall. Dates are set for distribution, yet no one knows how or from whom the needed funds will come. More recently, a few have committed to send a donation monthly. This is a great faith booster.

Many of you have gone on a food work camp to help with the sorting and distribution. Hundreds have given funds to provide the food. I wish that all of you could see the rooms with stacks of food from floor to ceiling. It is an emotional experience for me because I know that many have sacrificed to provide the food. Trucks line up in the street waiting to be loaded with food. Their delivery will be to the rain forest, the jungles, the mountains, the coast and to many poor villages near and far.

Prayers of thanksgiving and blessings are said for all those who have helped to provide the food. It takes work campers and nationals many hours to load the trucks.

The May distribution was the largest ever. More than two semi-truck loads of food were purchased in Quito. Later, the Lamberts went to Quevedo to purchase more food. When pastors and leaders come to Quito for training, they are fed from this fund. Families who receive food give at least 10% of their food to help others in their communities. They say, "Because God has blessed us with food, we want to give to others who have no one to help them."

I asked the Lamberts how many people receive the benefits of this food. They conferred together and said, "More than 5,000." (Between five and six thousand.)

The people do not receive more food than they did nine years ago. Sometimes they receive less. The amount given depends on funds available. The number of people who receive food continues to increase as the ministry increases. In Ecuador, wages are low; jobs hard to find. When there is no work, there is no food. They learned to stretch the food so there is something for the days when there is no work.

For those who may not have received mailings in the past and do not know the types of foods given, here is a partial list: rice, flour, sugar, powdered milk, oil, sardines, tuna, pasta, bouillon cubes, popcorn, beans, lentils, peas, barley rice, quinoa, oatmeal, fruit drink mix, and more. Food prices are about the same as in the U.S.

Thank you for giving the loaves and fish (flour, tuna and more). Because of you, the miracle goes on.

I will pray the Lord will bless your life with daily miracles.

My thanks to all of you for blessing my life with prayer gifts, friendship, and love. Please know that my love and prayers are ever with you.

Roma Lee

August, 2007

"He has scattered abroad his gifts to the poor." 2 Corinthians 9:9

Their faces glowed as Jorge and Marcela gave testimony of God's blessings. True gratitude flowed from within. How could they be so grateful when they have so little of what we call necessities?

Marcela said, "Before we knew the Lord we had nothing, but now, in Jesus, we have everything. We do not have comforts or things, but Jesus gives us peace and joy."

This family is not without suffering. Four months, Jorge had internal bleeding. Marcela has a very serious heart problem. One of their children has rheumatoid arthritis.

Jorge and Marcela are pastors in Quevedo, Ecuador. There is extreme poverty in Quevedo. Quevedo is located on the Pacific coastal plain, a very hot area of the country. With extreme poverty, jobs are hard to find, especially steady work that would provide food for a family. Even though Jorge works hard, there is never enough money for food and clothes. Usually, there is not enough money for the children to have lunch at school.

Marcela says, "Just when there is no more food, God sends us food through the Food Program. God is good. He even sends us clothes through work campers. See how nice we look! When people come to us asking us for food, we always share what we have. We pray everyday asking God to bless those who give to help provide food for us."

If you are receiving God's blessing, it may be because you have given to bless others. Perhaps, you are blessed because someone in a far away land prays every day for God to bless you.

If you can help provide food for Jorge, Marcela, their family and hundreds more, we need to receive donations by October 5. Food distribution will be November 1. Missionary Karen Lambert must begin ordering food by the first week of October.

My deepest thanks, love, and appreciation to each one of you who have given and continue to give to the Food for Ecuador Fund. As always, 100% of your donation goes to feed His children.

Blessings,
Roma Lee

November, 2007

The Hearts of People Cry Out to the Lord (Lamentations 2:18a)

Have you heard His children crying?
Have you heard His children praying?

I have heard them crying. Many of you have heard their cries. I have shared their need with you before. In the past eight years, some of you have helped many times to provide food for Ecuador. Some of you are hearing their cries for the first time. You will hear if you listen with your heart.

Eight years ago, El Niño devastated their land. Their crops were destroyed. Their government and economy collapsed. Many of them were without jobs or food. Some dug roots for food. They became malnourished, weak, and ill. Their faith was strong and they cried unto the Lord.

For some, life has improved. For the poor, life is still difficult. Jobs are hard to find. The rich do not help the poor and neither does the government.

I wish all of you could know our Ecuadorian people. They have great zeal and love for the Lord. Most of the churches are filled—or overfilled. I have seen people standing outside doorways and windows because there was no room inside.

They are a giving people. When they seem to have nothing, they find something to give. We give them food, and they divide it with others in need. When they have work and can buy food for their family, a portion is given to others.

They are a grateful people. Even in the worst of times, they always have a testimony or a song of praise because "God is with us." Daily they ask God to bless those in the United States who "bless us with food."

My heart is always touched and blessed by the miracle of the feeding of the hundreds. The miracle happens because you become the child with the lunch. You give your lunch to the Lord. He blesses your gift and hundreds are fed. Look, see them sitting down to be fed. Mothers weep for joy because there is food. Fathers help pass the food. Children reach out their hands. Jesus smiles because His children are fed.

The story is not just about hundreds being fed. It is about individuals. They each have a story. Mairo is one among the crowd. He has a story, a miracle story.

Mairo, a new Christian, left for work in the early morning. He had not gone far when two men stepped out of the darkness into his path. They held knives against him and demanded money. Mairo is poor. He had no money. The men stabbed him seven times. They threw him over a cliff into a deep canyon and left him to die. Mairo felt he was dying, then he felt arms lifting him up. When he opened his eyes, he was at the door of his home. His wife called for help to get him to a hospital. The doctors did nothing for him because he was dying—but Mairo didn't die. Later, they stitched and bound up his wounds. It was a long recovery, but he is alive and well today. How did Mairo get out of the canyon? No human could have brought him out. Blood covered the ground where he was stabbed. There was a trail of blood to the edge of the cliff but no trail of blood to his door. Surely, God sent angels to lift him up and carry him home.

Missionary Jon Lambert told us that Mairo is a good worker. He is willing to do hard labor, but jobs are difficult to find. He may have work for one week then have three weeks looking for work. How do Mairo, his wife, and two young children survive? They are part of the feeding miracle.

Thank you and God bless you,
Roma Lee

News From Distant Lands
March 3, 2009

I returned from Ecuador on February fifth. This camp was for food distribution. The amount of money given for the January food distribution was $85,470.00. Three and a half semi-truck loads of food were purchased. Praise be to the Lord! Just imagine the rejoicing when the people saw that amount of food. God bless each one of you who gave. God surely must smile as He sees your generous heart.

A few months ago, I received a call from Karen Lambert saying, "I have found someone to take your place with the food distribution ministry. Someone who has the same love and passion as you. She would like to come with you for the January distribution."

I have found this person to be sweet and caring. She has resources and contacts that I do not have. Every person has a different circle of friends and associates. I pray that God will bless her and enlarge this ministry through her efforts.

I have been working in Ecuador for more than twenty years. I have been working in the food distribution for ten years. The people there are some of the most loving, giving people in the world. They will forever have a special place in my heart.

This year is my sixtieth year in full-time ministry. Truly God is good! I am looking forward to some exciting things this year. I have worked in Peru since 1980. In the early years, I took building teams and medical tams to work mostly in the Lima area. For the past several years, I have taken groups to the Roma Lee Courvisier School to preach, teach, build classrooms, and do other ministries. The school is located in the desert near Reque, Peru. The beautiful school is like an oasis in the desert.

Many families in the community live in extreme poverty. They live in small shacks with dirt floors, no running water, and little food. In the past, the children attending school were served a plate of nourishing food at noon. It is difficult for children to study when they are hungry.

Last summer, I was disappointed when the 214 children at the R.L.C. (Roma Lee Courvisier School) were not receiving food at noon. I learned there were no more funds for this lunch program. I wanted to do something to help, but felt I could not add another country while endeavoring to raise funds for Ecuador. Now someone else will be helping the families in Ecuador.

God's call to me is, "Feed my lambs in Peru." Beginning this week, the children in Peru will receive a light breakfast and a hot meal for lunch. Thanks to all who have given to make this possible.

Remember, God really does love you…and I do too!

Roma Lee

Date Unknown

It is Christmastime in the city, in the country, and around the world!

Some of us have just experienced Christmas in Ecuador. Many of you shared in this experience even though you were not there.

We were there to purchase, sort, and load trucks with food to feed hundreds of people. You gave $40,579.71 to purchase food. Many families now have enough food staples to last several months. These families will receive additional food at Christmas time. This will include special treats such as cookies, raisins, Jell-O, extra milk, oatmeal, and other things.

All of these things are given because of God's amazing gift when He sent a Savior to the world. Because Christ has made a difference in our lives, we now make a difference for others.

I give personal thanks to all who have prayed for my health and given to my support You have made it possible for me to continue serving in missions. This has been a wonderful year in ministry. For this, I give thanks to God. Without His blessings, nothing of eternal value can be accomplished.

I give thanks to you who have prayed, given, or gone to a world in need. May God's blessings be multiplied in your lives a hundred-fold.

Wishing You Happy Holidays!

Blessings and love,
Roma Lee

A Side Trip

Correspondence from Jon and Karen Lambert reveals the deep need for food in Ecuador.

January 20, 2006

Dear Roma Lee and Donors,

We once again want to thank you all for participating in the Food for Ecuador program. Many of you have been here as we purchase, divide, and distribute the truckloads of life-sustaining food. However, most of you have not been able to see this firsthand. There are so many stories we would love to share with you about the difference your gifts have meant to the Ecuadorian church, but there are two that we especially want to share.

A week after the food was distributed; we were attending a special service at the Zabala church in Quito. Pastor Martha invited a time of testimonies and a young mother followed by two young boys walked to the front of the sanctuary. The worn look on the mother's face spoke volumes of her trials. She began to share that her husband recently abandoned the family and left them without income. He hated the fact that she was going to church and would no longer follow him to the bars. You see, there are no social programs in Ecuador for the poor or abandoned. You are on your own. The situation for this family had grown desperate. Their cupboard was bare.

With tears, this mother said, "Then we went to church and were told that food was arriving!"

After the service, one of her boys, Louis, came up to us and hugged us so tightly. "Thank you for saving us," he said.

On the costal plains of Ecuador, life has been extremely hard this year. The people there are in the worst drought in over one hundred years. All the crops have failed and the cost of fruits and vegetables has soared. Many are out of work because most jobs are agriculture related. The Quevedo, Concordia, and Tonsupa churches have been greatly affected by the drought. In Quevedo, the pastor's wife, Marcela, has also been very ill this year. Between the high food costs and the doctor's bills, the Arroba family was drained of all resources.

When we were buying the food for them, Marcela began to cry as the warehouse worker named off the quantities of food purchased.

"You cannot know what this means to us," Marcela said.

Jesus asked Peter,
"Do you love me?"...
..."Feed my lambs."

Jon and Karen Lambert
Missionaries to Ecuador

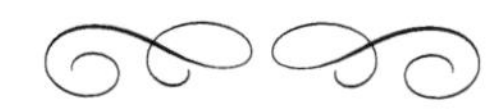

A Letter of Thanks *(Date Unknown)*

Dear Roma Lee and Donors,

Once you have witnessed the distribution of food to hungry families, you have scenes in your mind that never fade. My comments are a series of memories.

First, the single mother from Victoria's church who came to church that night not expecting to see North Americans nor receive anything material. Watching her and her children drag the three huge sacks of food into the night with tears streaming as they left was almost too much. You see, there was no food in their house and this mother had worried all day what they were going to eat for the next week. She was overwhelmed, then tears became sobs, and then she just broke down in thankful joy.

Next, I remember the families from the Comite church. On this night we stood in a second-floor window and watched as four families, talking and laughing, made their way down four different streets that radiated from the church, each lugging great sacks of food. It was like fingers of love spreading across that Quito neighborhood. One small boy, about six years old, lagged behind pushing a box full of rice and flour toward his parents and home. They would call back to him from farther down the street. Finally, he too disappeared into the night.

Finally, a family from the Pamplona church, deep in the coastal rain forest, loaded a horse with enough basic food to last them for up to six months, and we watched them head out on the three-hour horse trail to their little settlement. How wide, how far, how deep is the love of Christ. It reaches to the ends of the earth. Even to a hungry family in the deepest part of a South American rainforest.

Thank you all. You have blessed hundreds of families more than you will even know.

Jon and Karen Lambert
Missionaries to Ecuador

E-mail messages from the Lamberts in Ecuador, Monday, March 5, 2007.

From Karen: What a joy it is to be able to share with those in need—both physically and spiritually. The food program has been such a blessing for the church here in Ecuador. God has blessed the food, and has brought people to Him through these efforts. It has been a blessing to watch as mothers have come to receive their portion, and have wept telling us that they and their children came to church with nothing to eat because there was no food in the house.

One of the great joys for us has been watching the spiritual growth of the people through your giving as well. Sister Martha, the pastor of our Zabala church, came to me several years ago and said that most of the women who attend services are not married to Christian men. The situation at home is difficult at best and there is no way their husbands will let them tithe on the money he brings home. Most of these women have very little education, so they earn almost nothing. The ladies had come to Sister Martha worried about how they could tithe. She challenged them to put some of that food aside for God and see if God will still fill their needs.

She set a "Love Basket" at the front of the sanctuary. The ladies brought in their very small portions of food. When the basket got full, they would pray together and let God lead them to someone in the community that did not know Him and was in need. As they took the food and witnessed to people, they saw lives changed and real spiritual growth take place. The ladies were so amazed. They told Sister Martha that they were shocked that their families still had enough to eat. What a tool for growth in faith and trusting God's Word even when we don't see how we can follow Him.

It wasn't long before Sister Martha came to me with a big smile and said, "TWO! We had to set out two love baskets today!" God used the food program to feed the bodies and souls of His children and to call more souls to Him.

From Jon: Roma Lee asked me to write about the food program and how it has helped the church in Ecuador. I thought about the first time food was given and the difference that help is still making today.

Let me tell you about Samuel, the pastor's son at our Meridiano church, deep in the northwestern Ecuadorian rain forest. When we delivered the first food to Meridiano, Samuel was four years old. Samuel's stomach was distended, his hair had a reddish tint, and he was almost lifeless. He stared at us from his doorway with a blank expression, as if his mind was empty.

Last month at our monthly pastors' meeting in Quito, Samuel came bounding in with his father. Now almost a teenager, Samuel is a bright, vibrant, typical boy. He is a bit small for his age, but his mind is sharp. I thought about what would have happened to Samuel if his family had not been receiving the help of the food. We constantly come in contact with malnourished children. Most cannot function in school and have permanent learning disabilities. We used to see them in our churches, but not as much anymore. It seems to have drastically declined at the same time the food program began.

A Side Trip

The Cayambe Indians

The Cayambe Indians of today are descendants of the pre-Inca Kayambi people. The Kayambi were resistant to Inca expansion and were ultimately conquered by Huayna Capac after a bloody twenty-year war. At that time, the Kayambi people adopted the Kichwa language. Not long afterwards, in the sixteenth century, the first Spanish *conquistadores* arrived in the region. Kichwa survives in some of the hamlets today, while in others it has given way to Spanish.

The area hosts numerous flower plantations whose products are destined for the overseas cut flower market. Toxic inputs and unsafe practices associated with these plantations have damaged the local environment and created health problems among the workers.[3]

3. Wikipedia.com, s.v. "Cayambe, Ecuador," http://en.wikipedia.org/wiki/Cayambe,_Ecuador. Used by permission under Creative Commons Attribution-ShareAlike License.

Top: Food ready for distribution.
Bottom: Roma Lee crossing the swinging bridge at Bela Vista.

Top: Ribbon cutting ceremony for the Santa Clara church with Delia and Paula Rodriguez.
Bottom: An Ecuadorian ready to take her much needed food home.

CHAPTER 9

Peru

Larry and Jeanne Alexander from the Pleasant Prairie Church of God in Kansas were serving as missionaries in Pullcalpa, Peru. Roma Lee took two groups to work with them to construct buildings. On one particular trip, the group spent the night in a hotel in Lima since there were no air flights from Lima to Pullcalpa that evening. Roma Lee contacted the national leaders, Solomon and Carmen Cabanillas. Their daughter Clara and son-in-law Willie Baraybar were involved in the work in Peru with the Cabanillas. On the following day, Roma Lee and the group spent the day with the Cabanillas and Baraybars in Lima. When she visited the mountainside community of Caja de Agua, she became aware of the need for a church to minister to the poorest of the poor. Her intent was to visit Lima for just the one day while waiting for an airplane, but God pricked her heart and she began a ministry to the Lima area that engulfed many years.

Roma Lee met Ken Biron when she was speaking at South Side Church of God in St. Louis, Missouri, pastored by Ralph Shupe.

While viewing the slides of Peru, Ken heard God clearly say, "Pay attention, you will be there one day."

Ken began going on work camps with Roma Lee. His heart was touched by the needs of the Peruvian people, especially the children. Ken began working with a child sponsorship program. During this time in Peruvian history, the Shining Path was active, kidnapping priests, nuns, and other religious leaders. The Shining Path bombed power plants and water towers, which left many people without power and water for long periods of time. They destroyed bridges over the river so people could not get to work from one side of the river to the other.

Roma Lee took a few work camps during this time, until it became too dangerous to take large groups into the country. There were times when the groups were stopped by police several times between the airport and the missionary's home. The work campers were fearful that the police guards would trump up charges against them and they would be detained in Peruvian prisons. Roma Lee recalled the anxiety and fear from the work campers when armed police guards stopped the bus, boarded it, and demand to see passports. She did not take groups to Peru for a few months, but she continued to go herself to take funds for the work. It was a violent time in the country.

In addition to working with Willie and Clara Baraybar, she worked with a local pastor Jose Arbildo and his wife Gladys. Gladys absolutely loved Christmas. She did not have a Christmas tree, so she would put a paper tree on her wall and draw ornaments on it. Roma Lee purchased an artificial Christmas tree and ornaments for Gladys. Along with Roma Lee, the family spent the night decorating the beautiful tree and listening to Christmas music on tape. The Shining Path bombings began. As the vibrations from the explosions shook the house, the family continued decorating the tree with the music turned up a bit louder. No one showed any sign of fear, not even their young daughter.

The remnants of the war lingered long after the war was over. Dangerous land mines remained in the countryside. One of the young girls from the church became a teacher. The girl took her students on a walk and stepped on a landmine. Even though she lost one leg in the explosion, she continued to teach.

Ken Biron's acute awareness of the lack of education for children in Peru led him to start the Roma Lee Courvisier School in Reque. Roma Lee continued taking work camps to Reque to build buildings and provide teacher training, as well as raising funds to feed not only the children at the school but people in neighboring communities where Sunday schools were located.

The Sunday school in New Reque, Peru rotated from house to house. Sometimes the women cooked breakfast for the gatherings. The breakfast consisted of an egg and cheese sandwich, a sweet potato sandwich or oatmeal and a soy drink. If an afternoon meal was served, it consisted of locally grown vegetables such as carrots, squash or beans and served with rice, chicken, turkey or duck.

On this particular day, as was the custom, a room was cleared of its meager furnishings in a house for the services of the day. There were about twenty-five children packed into the little room with a dirt floor for Sunday school.

The women brought their own stoves for cooking and prepared a meal for the anticipated hundreds of people for the afternoon meal. The Peruvians had little food at home, so these meals were important to the well-being of both children and adults.

The leaders planned a wonderful day, including putting up a canopy and preparing a program. The men brought guitars and keyboards for the program. The pastor from the local church shared the gospel message.

The pastor then said, "Children, go home and get your parents. We will have a service for them and we will eat together."

The children ran home to get parents, family members, and friends. A group of bystanders outside the house had observed the Sunday school for the children.

Roma Lee said to Ken, "Please go and invite all of the people standing outside. They must come to the service to hear the gospel and eat with us."

More than five hundred people heard the gospel preached that day in Peru and ate a nourishing meal.

An old man who looked to be about ninety years old came to the gathering. It is very rare for a person to live to ninety in a third-world country. Roma Lee made it a point to sit beside the man. His clothes were dirty, ragged, and hanging on his frail body. He looked hungry; in fact, he quickly consumed the meal of rice, vegetables, and a few pieces of chicken.

She recalled, "My heart was greatly moved by the old man."

Roma Lee saw the old man hobbling toward a dirt road as he left the gathering.

"Please, someone go stop the old man. We must give him some food to take home. He is so hungry," Roma Lee said with urgency in her voice. The old man graciously took the extra food and continued on his way home.

When Roma Lee returned to the States, she could not forget the old man. God impressed her that she must find him again, where he lived, and learn his needs.

When she returned to Peru, she said to Ken with an urgent tone in her voice, "I have not been able to forget the old man; I must find him!"

She and Ken, along with several work campers, loaded a pickup truck with food and began searching. In a short time, they found him in a humble home with few furnishings. The home soon became a place of worship as they sat on rough wooden benches, leaned their backs against the wall, and sang "How Great Thou Art" in Spanish and English simultaneously. The old man removed his floppy old hat in reverence to God as they sang and prayed together.

The old man shared, "My wife died twenty-two years ago. I'm lonely and just waiting for God to come and get me."

"I saw a tear in his eye and I believe that God smiled," Roma Lee recounted.

God's purpose of sending Roma Lee to find the old man was not just to provide food for him. She and Ken discovered that the old man's daughter, Rosa, was dying from cancer. She was lying in a dark room on a dirt floor with the only light coming from a small window since the house had no electricity. Rosa, weak and in pain, was bleeding and had no control of her body functions. She was in need of medicine and diapers. Not only did the father and daughter live in the house, but so did the granddaughter and her two children.

Rosa quickly shared that both she and her father were Christians. After a time of prayer, Ken left to get medicine and other needed supplies. On the next trip to Peru, Roma Lee heard the news that Rosa had died.

"You have to go find the people in need. If we seek them, God will help us find them," stated Roma Lee. "I just had to find the old man. I still do not know his name, but God knows it. When God comes to get him, He will call the old man by name. God knows each of us by name. When he calls us to help His children in need, He calls us by name. Listen for your name."

Adjacent to the Roma Lee Courvisier School in Reque, Peru, is the police academy. Ken befriended the personnel at the academy; however, no one had ever been invited to the grounds of the academy. As usual, when there seems to be no way of contact with people, Roma Lee is blessed with doors of opportunity. The North American group led by Roma Lee was given the honor of an invitation to the academy. Knowing this prior to the trip, Roma Lee collected patches from police departments across the United States.

The security at the Dayton International Airport [Ohio] stopped her with multiple questions about the number of police patches that she was carrying onto the plane. She simply explained that the patches were a good will gesture from all over the United States for a police academy in the remote desert of Peru.

The mutual friendship between the academy and the school continues to the present.

In Her Own Words

June 1990
Lima, Peru

I saw an angel in a pink dress. She was such a tiny little girl and only a few knew she ever existed! Her name was Garada. She was born in a home of poverty. Her family lived in the mountains in northern Peru. She never had any of the comforts of life that most of us think are necessary. She not only had the handicap of poverty, she had an even greater handicap—that of deafness.

It must have been a frightening experience when she was barely five years old to leave her parents and go to live with her aunt in a community near Lima. The aunt, in whose small house she was to live, already had eight children. They lived near a Christian school and home for deaf children. For three years, Garada walked the few blocks each day to attend the school. This year, Garada was eight years old.

On June twenty-fifth, a group of North Americans arrived at the deaf school to paint the dining hall and kitchen. We were greeted with lots of smiles, hugs, and kisses.

It is always a heart-touching experience to walk into their silent world, yet in no other place do I feel a stronger love or greater awareness of the presence of Him who said, "Suffer the children come unto me, and forbid them not, for of such is the kingdom of heaven" (Matthew 19:14 KJV).

In addition to the painters in our group, there were women to help the children make small crafts. The children were thrilled to have their dining hall and kitchen painted, but best of all was to have someone reaching out to them with loving hands and arms. Each day was more exciting than Christmas or birthdays because there were treats, balls, balloons, and young people to teach them new games—and plenty of hugs to go around!

On the last full day of Garada's life on earth, she must have hurried home from school very fast with a smiling face and shining eyes to show her aunt the craft she had made—a pretty mobile to hang.

Early the next morning she was on her way to school anticipating the joy of being with her new friends again. In her deafness, she did not hear the bus that hit her. That day, great sadness filled the hearts of children and workers. Cheeks were wet with tears and hearts felt empty and lonely.

In the evening, I went to visit Garada's aunt. There was little furniture in the small house. By candlelight, I could see the crude wooden table covered with a white cloth. On the table lay a little pink dress waiting for the body of Garada to be returned to the home. There were no parents present to grieve for her. There was no way to contact them in their home in the mountains. They were unaware that their child was dead.

As I rode back to Lima in a taxi, there was time to think, to pray, and to grieve—to grieve not just for the loss of a child, but to grieve because she had only known poverty and life in the silent world of the deaf and separation from parents.

There was time also to give thanks. Thanks for an aunt who shared not from her bounty, but from her poverty…for teachers and workers who gave her a language, an opportunity for learning, and the message of Jesus and His love. I felt joy and comfort in the knowledge that this child who was born in poverty and lived in poverty was now enjoying all the riches of heaven.

On this day as she entered the gates of Heaven into the loving arms of Jesus, it would not have been a strange experience. For she had already felt His love in the loving arms of Christian workers. It was almost as though she stepped from our arms to His, and to think that the first sounds she ever heard was the sound of angels singing!!

Our group gave a love offering to bury Garada. The next day when our work was finished, we went to the aunt's house to leave our gift and to place flowers by the little white wooden box that held the body of an angel…in a pink dress.

I felt the presence of One not seen. There was a loving touch on each heart. I could almost see His face. There were tears in His eyes and He smiled when He said, "Inasmuch as you have done it unto one of the least of these my brethren, you have done it unto me" (Matthew 25:40b KJV).

Roma Lee

Lima, Peru
Sunday, April 19, 1991, Easter Sunday

Dear One,

Would you take time to come with me for a while? I know it will be later when you receive these words, but today as I think of you and pray for you, you seem very close.

Today is Easter Sunday and I want to share this day with you. Darkness still hovers over the streets, but I am awake and there is time to read the Easter story before the 6:00 a.m. service begins. I wonder if that Easter, so long ago, began much as it has here today, with dogs barking, cocks crowing, and trouble in the city. On that first Easter while darkness still hovered over the streets, a dim light flickered in a window where women were preparing for a special mission that day. I try to imagine what it would have been like to have been with the women on their way to the tomb. I tremble with excitement at the thought. Had I been with them, I would have lifted my skirt a little above my sandals and ran! (Surely those guards at the tomb would have been no more of a problem than those in customs.) The women were not afraid, because their hearts and minds were fixed on their mission.

Now, as this Easter begins to dawn, I make my way with other Christians to church to worship and praise our risen Lord. Young people are leading the service. Their faces are aglow with the beauty of Christ. There are many young people in the service. Some of them are new Christians. Some were baptized only last week. Today, the Lilly of the Valley blooms in their hearts. The Bright and Morning Star gives new light upon their path. Together we sing, "Because He lives, I can face tomorrow."[1]

---

1. "Because He Lives." Lyrics by Gloria Gaither and William J. Gaither. © 1971 by William J. Gaither.

It is a heart-lifting service. We are blessed by the Spirit and the Word. After the service ends, we linger for fellowship and sharing. There are many hugs given and received. I hold one mother in my arms while she weeps and tells me of problems in her home. Then a young mother comes with joy to place her newborn baby in my arms.

It is time now for a journey across town to visit in the home of dear friends. We will ride the public bus. It will take about forty-five minutes to one hour to arrive at our destination. The smell of diesel fuel is heavy, but I don't mind for I have pleasant memories associated with that smell. The buses are always packed—to say crowded is an understatement. Sometimes, it is a place to make a new friend. Always, it is an inexpensive cultural experience. The traffic is impossible to describe. (Especially now, since many streets are closed by the military.) With five lanes of traffic on three-lane streets, and no one observing traffic lights or signs, it is the time and place for prayer. I am not as concerned about traffic problems as other scenes from the bus window. As I look at the masses of people (more than eight million live in Lima), I wonder about their lives. Do they know Jesus? Have they ever heard the message of salvation? I look at their faces. I see much pain and sorrow. I see hunger as some search through garbage heaps. There are children in rags, much too small to be on the streets alone. Soldiers with guns line the streets, and tanks surround the government buildings. Only a few days ago, their president fired the vice president and congress and declared himself as sole leader of the country. The Shining Path terrorist group has moved their headquarters into Lima. Bombings have increased in the city. As I watch the people on the street I wonder (as they do) about their future.

We arrive at the home of friends. Loving hearts and hands have prepared a wonderful meal of typical Peruvian foods.

So much kindness and love is given to us that I feel I must be standing on holy ground.

Now come with me to the evening service of Easter celebration. A large crowd has gathered. They have come from several nearby areas. Tonight, we are in a special service. It is a service to remember what Christ has done for us. It is a service of Communion and a time to wash the feet of others as a symbol of our desire to be a servant to all in His Name.

The one keeling to wash my feet is the one whom I held in my arms this morning as she wept for needs in her home. Now, one of the least and greatest is ministering unto me.

As I kneel before one that I love and have often prayed for, I remember experiences of the past. I remember the many times I have visited her home to leave gifts of food and clothes. She lives in a shack and has never known the comfort of a good bed or the luxury of a bathroom. There has never been enough clothes or food for her twelve children. Often, I have felt sadness and frustration because she showed no interest in spiritual things. I knew she taught her children to be beggars—perhaps even thieves. I knew she took advantage of North Americans by charging three times the value of small handmade items. I knew these things, but I knew also that Jesus' love and power are greater than all our sins. Tonight, that love shines on her face. The miracle of a changed life is a reality. I give thanks for the privilege of washing her feet. Feet that are tired, rough, and dirty. My eyes are blurred with tears, but those brown feet look like your feet, Lord.

Darkness falls. Again. Easter has ended. Soon I will return home to a place of reasonable safety. There are no soldiers with guns on my street. Tanks do not surround our city buildings. No buildings in my neighborhood have been bombed by terrorists. I will not have to wonder if tomorrow or next week I will have food to eat. But this I know: I cannot eat my bread alone. For

Jesus said, "Go, feed my lambs, feed my sheep" (John 21:15, 16 KJV).

May the fullness of His love and blessings by yours…

Because He Lives!
Roma Lee

Sunday, November 15, 1992
Lima, Peru

No one ran to greet us as we entered the gate. We walked toward a large building, which was once used as a hospital. Now, the faded green paint was peeling and everything in sight was a witness to neglect. The buildings and surrounding grounds are now the site of a lepers' colony.

Shy children peeked around corners and from doorways of small shacks. We made our way to a room in the main building where Sunday school was held. Several children attend the Sunday school faithfully. No adults had ever attended. I stood in the doorway and looked out on a people in despair. I saw a leper with only one leg hobbling across the grounds on crutches. There was another in a wheelchair. As he came closer, I saw that one leg was missing up to a protruding stub at the knee. The stub had large open ulcers. His fingers were gone, only knobs remained and those covered with white scales.

Some things remain much the same from the time Jesus walked on earth until today. The lepers are still shunned and live apart from the rest of society. The children of lepers attend school far enough away from home so that they are not known.

Where they are known, they are shunned and discriminated against.

The pain of lepers and their families pierced my heart. I desired so much that they would come and hear God's Word.

I wanted to go to them, to touch them in the name of the Lord and to say, "Come and hear the good news." There was little time before the service, but I knew that I must go to them—even if they refused to come. So, my God and I walked together and God did a wonderful thing.

I did not feel like a stranger in a foreign land. I felt like one who had come home and someone was waiting. I saw pictures of their children and pictures of happy family times. I heard about loved ones who had died. I gave the invitation to "come." I knew (and I think they knew) it was not my invitation, but His. And then I realized God only let me come along to watch Him work.

Soon it was time for the service to begin. And they came! All that were invited came, five women, four men, youth and children. There was the man on crutches, one in the wheelchair, and another almost blind; the lame, the blind, they came!

The face of my new friend, Luz, glowed. It did not matter that her clothes were tattered—not even the large hole in the knee of her black pants. She seemed filled with joy and pride as she sat with her teenage daughter, niece, and nephew. During the singing, Luz left. I wondered if she would return. Very quickly she was back with a tambourine in her hand, which she gave to her teenage nephew Carlos to play.

I watched the one without fingers clap his stubby hands together as we sang praises to the Lord. At that moment, I would not have been surprised to see One in our midst who looked like the Son of God. Surely to those who have sat in darkness and isolation for so long, a ray of light from God's Word shined upon their hearts (Isaiah 9:2 KJV).

Sunday, November 22, 1992
Lima, Peru

There were happy faces to greet us today as we entered the gate and walked toward the old building that was once Guia Hospital. Five of us were loaded with gifts (a special gift for each mother), food (125 ham and cheese sandwiches, 155 bananas, bags of cookies and gallons of raspberry drink) and a Christmas tree.

I carried a few bright ornaments. It was a happy time as children helped hang bright colored balls on the tree. Probably none of the families will have a tree in their home. There are eighteen families in the lepers' colony. Sixty or more children and youth are a part of these family units. It was wonderful to see again those who came last week and to get to know more of these precious people. I wish you could know them too. Let me introduce you to some of them.

Sandra is a teenager. She is pretty, friendly, and soft-spoken. She lives in the lepers' colony with her aunt. To me, it seemed especially sad for one not born to a leper's family to have circumstances that put her there. Sandra whispered to me that she would like to take me on a walk to see others.

Maximiliana is quiet and gentle with a loving spirit. She wanted to be sure everyone had food, even wanting to share her food.

Jose, not as handicapped as some, has a bright and cheerful spirit and enjoys talking.

Hernan is severely handicapped. One leg is gone and his fingers already eaten away by leprosy. He expressed so beautifully the gratitude of his heart for what they had received.

Luz, excited, grateful and outgoing, wanted to help with everything. She wanted to take me to the rest of her family. She would be a good "take charge" leader.

Nelly seems the most self-conscious with her deformed hands. She is quiet, yet stood and spoke words of gratitude on behalf of the entire group.

So you see, the lepers and their families are real people, people who need someone to care, someone to share, and someone to pray.

Jesus cared and loved the lepers when He walked on earth, and He cares today.

"Now when John had heard in the prison the words of Christ, he sent two of his disciples and said unto him, 'Art thou He that should come, or do we look for another?' Jesus answered and said unto them, 'Go and show John again those things which ye do hear and see: the blind receive their sight, the lame walk, the lepers are cleansed, and the deaf hear, the dead are raise up, and the poor have the gospel preached to them'" (Matthew 11:2–5 KJV).

We do not look for another. A Savior has come.

"Surely He hath borne our grief, carried our sorrows: yet we did esteem him stricken, smitten of God and afflicted. But He was wounded for our transgressions, He was bruised for our iniquities: the chastisement of our peace was upon Him: and with His stripes we are healed" (Isaiah 53:4–5 KJV).

Let us go and tell!
Roma Lee

Lima Peru—Christmas, 1994

From My Heart to You,

You are in my heart and mind today as you so often are.

Many times this year when I have been riding in a river boat through the heart of a jungle, walking dusty trails, climbing mountains, holding a child, giving Bibles, praying with the dying, giving gifts to the deaf or feeding the lepers…I think of you.

I think of your sacrifice to send me to the mission fields. I think of your labors and giving to provide churches, clinics, and schools for those who have no funds to help themselves. I remember the labors of love from doctors, dentists, and nurses to relieve the suffering of many. I think of your donations of medicine, food, clothes, and Bibles. Always, I remember love when I think of you.

There are so many places I would like to take you, for I know you would be blessed to see how many lives are touched through you.

In heart and mind, come with me today to Caja de Agua in Lima, Peru.

Walk through the door into a house of poverty. We sense that it is a home where love abides and God's presence is felt. We are led to a small bedroom. There lying on a mattress with no sheet was a heap of bones with skin stretched tightly over the bones. Small bony hands are so immovable they could have been chiseled from stone. The fingers are twisted one over the other and then drawn into the palms of his hands. There are sores on his legs, and the toes are twisted as his fingers are and then drawn under his feet. He has lain upon this bed for four years. But oh, look at his face—it glows! There is radiance about him. His eyes are weak, but clear and alert. You can see his heart in his eyes. His mouth is drawn slightly to the side. There is almost no movement of his lips when he tries to speak. He greets us. His wife gently takes him in her arms and lifts him to the side of the bed. With one hand and arm, she holds him. With the other hand, she strokes his hair and face. A teenage daughter sits beside him also. She keeps patting him and speaking soft words, always smiling and sometimes giggling as they share their special communication. There is nothing but pure love and adoration in the eyes of the wife and daughter. You feel he must have always been a loving husband and father.

He begins to sing. The words are hard to understand, but we recognize the songs. We join him in singing, "I Am a Child of God" (Barney Warren); "Onward Christian Soldiers" (Sabine Barying-Gould), and "What a Friend We Have in Jesus" (Joseph Scriven).

He quotes scriptures. John 3:16 is his favorite, *"Porque de tal manera amo Dios al mundo, que ha dado a su Hijo unigenito, para que todo aquel. Que en el cree, no se pierada, mas tenga vida eternal."* "For God so loved the world that He gave his only begotten Son that whosoever believeth in Him should not perish, but have everlasting life" (KJV). The message is the same in any language.

After sharing many scriptures, the daughter is instructed to prepare food for us. I follow her to the barren kitchen. I see only two or three carrots and a green vegetable. I assure her we have just eaten lunch before coming to her home and that we have no hunger.

We learned that a wheelchair is the greatest desire and need of this husband and father. When given money to purchase a wheelchair, his response was thanksgiving and praise to God.

His first words to us were "Now I can go to church."

We leave gifts for Christmas and money for food. We say prayers and goodbyes. We begin our walk down the mountain.

With hearts full of emotion, eyes moist, we ponder what we have seen and felt. We are more aware than ever that things have little or nothing to do with love, peace, and joy.

We are made to wonder about ourselves and others who take so lightly the privilege and opportunity to attend church services. We consider our responsibility (we the stuffed) to the starving.

We will walk many paths in the new year. Perhaps, sometimes we will walk together, sometimes far apart. But please know that I think of you with gratitude, love, and prayers.

Someone has written the words, that as a new year dawns, I make my prayer, "Give me windows to look out, and doors to go beyond."[2]

Merry Christmas! May God bless all your days as you walk...

In His love,
Roma Lee

September 1996

I would like to share a recent experience with you.

For 15 years, I have worked with and loved the people of Lima, Peru. God still allows me to walk in new places. Come into the streets with me; see the faces.

Children stopped their play and stood back against old buildings that once had been used for businesses. Now they stood like tombs in a cemetery. Brown eyes stared at the strange

2. Source unknown.

woman with very fair skin and blue eyes. As with children everywhere, they soon responded to a smile, a touch, and a hug.

The faces of women standing in the doorways or on the street were pictures of despair. They live without bathroom facilities or any modern conveniences. They are surrounded by piles of trash, garbage, and open sewage.

Men sat crouched in corners and along the street. As cold wind whipped dust in their faces, they pulled dirty rags closer around their bodies. A man hurrying down the street wearing a well-worn bright red cape, looked like bones walking.

We walked down a narrow passage to a small room where Christians meet to pray, sing, and study the Bible. I felt welcome to share in their fellowship. Lillie, the leader of the group, had once been a drug addict, as had others in the group. Lillie now devotes her life to helping others find deliverance and new life through Jesus Christ.

After prayer, Lillie and three other women invited me to join them in community visitation. Lillie is fearless, bold, and caring.

As we walked down another narrow passage, I remembered the scripture that speaks of the "valley of the shadow of death" (Psalm 23:4 KJV).

I thought, "This is the alley of the shadow of death."

On either side of the passage were small rooms. To step through the doorways, we had to step over an open trench flowing with sewage. The stench was worse than any I had ever experienced. Children play in this passage. A toddler stumbled into the sewage. I wondered what diseases the children carry in their bodies. At the end of the passage was a small courtyard. We began to sing songs that all children in Latin America know and love, especially "Alabare" (Jose Pagan and Manual Alonso). Eight children and four adults joined us in singing. There was an Unseen Presence in our midst. I felt His gentle touch. Our small gifts were given in His name. The Word was placed in their hands. Many hugs later, we were on our way to the next stop.

On that day, I did not take a picture. It would not have been safe to carry a camera. I will not forget their faces, for I carry a picture in my heart. The picture is clear except the center is slightly smudged where Jesus' tears fell.

Thank you for praying, giving, and sending me to the "least of these."

With love and gratitude,
Roma Lee

Peru—1999

What is the worth of a centimos Peruvian coin? Not much. No one treasures this small coin. It is seldom used. It would hardly be worth picking up from the street. No one would care if it were lost.[3]

What is the worth of three Peruvian children? To the government, not much. There is no help for them. Few know they exist.

Danny, Dora, and Sandy Lopez Villegas are beautiful and loving children, created in the image of God. In their young lives, they have already known more pain, hunger, and hardships than most of us will ever know. They have been deaf since birth. They were born not only into the silent, lonely world of deafness, but also into a home of poverty.

3. Editor's note: A five centimos coin was glued to each newsletter.

At age eight, Danny began attending EFATA Christian School for the deaf. He is still a student there. Dora and Sandy are also students at the school.

The children have yet another handicap. The loss of sight. They will be totally blind without treatment. There is no cure for this affliction. But with medical treatment, the length of time they can have sight might be extended for years.

Danny is the oldest. His vision is greatly affected. By late afternoon, he can only see people as shadows. Danny is an artist. I am amazed at his God-given talent. His sight is better earlier in the day, but even then, he must paint with his eyes close to the canvas.

I do not understand the medical terms and explanations of the health problems of these children. I know that without medical treatment, the children will be totally blind. The cost of the medicine needed is $300 a month, $100 per child.

What are three Peruvian children worth? Are they worth giving sight to them? Would anyone notice if three deaf and blind children were lost on the street?

I thought you would want to know about Danny, Dora, and Sandy. Later, I will tell you the rest of the story. Maybe it will be a good story…probably that depends on all of us!

Roma Lee

Update on Church Planting in Ventanilla, Peru—2000

Willie and Clara Baraybar began their ministry in Ventanilla teaching a small group in a yard! The church in the yard grew.

They made a place for worship with plywood walls and a straw mat roof. Soon this place was filled with people.

Churches in the U.S. have responded to help plant a church in Ventanilla. Lots were purchased; work campers have gone each month to help build. It has been exciting to see brick walls going up and cement floors poured. Several men from the community have been working with the North Americans. Each of these men, except one, are now Christians. Work campers have had a great impact for Christ. Workers with children told Bible stories, sang songs, played games and gave lots of hugs. One group of medical workers gave relief to 350–400 persons each day through their touch of love, prayer, and medicine.

During the work camps, more than thirty adults made decisions for Christ. More than eighty children now attend the Sunday school. Work continues on the building. I will be going back to Ventanilla soon.

On August 2, just before returning to Peru, I fell in my home. My back was broken and I have a crushed vertebrae. There is a great deal of pain with this injury. I am in a body brace that extends from my neck to over my hips. I am thankful to be doing well and able to travel. (Daughter/Editor's comment: As you all know, she will always tell us she is doing, "Just fine!" The one fear she has is that others will think that she is going to quit. But most of us know her well enough to understand that something like a broken back won't stop her. However, she truly does need special prayer during this time. The pain has been intense. We are trusting that with lots of bed rest, she will be in less pain by the time she leaves to take the money to Ecuador. Her passion to take the love of Christ to those in need keeps her going!)

It has been a wonderful blessing to work with many of you these past few weeks and months. I thank God for you.

My deep gratitude to all who have given support to me personally. I know that many of you pray daily for me, for the work camps, and for special needs on the mission field. It is because of your faithfulness in prayer that God has given strength, healing and salvation to many.

Thank you for giving to the Lord!
Roma Lee

Work camp to Reque, Peru
Summer 2001

(Among the group of twenty-three work campers with me in Reque, Peru, last summer was my niece Sandra Courvisier. The following article is Sandra's report of the work camp. Editor's Note: Sandra committed her life to the Lord in Nicaragua on a work camp, she was baptized on a work camp to Ecuador, and she wrote this article on a work camp in Peru.)

As a volunteer, each and every work camper goes to "bless" the children and the people with their hearts and their skills. Yet when you ask any work camper who returned to Florida, Kentucky, Ohio, Missouri, Texas, Oklahoma, and California respectively, they will tell you that God returned the blessing individually more than anyone would have imagined!

Following our arrival, blessings came to all of us the first day when the children performed a program in support of Peru's Independence Day celebration. The children dressed in typical, traditional attire for the performance, and each class performed a different song and dance routine. Included in the performance were some of the animals from Noah's ark!

Following the performance that day, several work campers began skilled labor to assist in the construction of foundations and walls for new classrooms. Concurrently, some campers visited the children and teachers in their classrooms, while others began sorting over twenty suitcases of donations. And what donations they were! In support of every traveler, people provided a myriad of goods, including school supplies, Bibles, clothes, sewing kits, toiletry bags, crafts, treats, and toys for the children.

Speaking of gifts, Christ continued to bless everyone with a weekend evangelistic crusade. One of our work campers led the evangelistic services Friday, Saturday, and Sunday evenings. Praise the Lord, many accepted Christ as Savior, and some who were ill were healed. Several from our group shared their personal testimonies, which was an absolute inspiration. As for the North Americans, many of us commented, among ourselves, how the words shared in the service spoke to us right where we are presently with Him in our lives. This serves as a testimony to the fact that we're certain everyone was blessed during the crusade!

Also, in support of the teachers, another of our very own skilled educators spoke to and encouraged the teachers in their approach to teaching the children. At that time, all teachers were presented with gift bags, compliments, love, and respect for their contribution to changing the lives of children that have such great needs.

In my experience, and for each and every work camper, the trip ends the same. We think about our own needs in shame compared to the needs of the Latin Americans we come in contact with.

We begin to ask ourselves, "What else can I do to help these people when I get home?"

The answer is always the same: Pray for the ministry, sponsor a child, collect donations, encourage others to sponsor or travel, and, for goodness sake, come back for another work camp trip! In closing, my only hope is that sharing our experience will inspire and help others to understand how God blesses every aspect of a work camp adventure!

Sandra Courvisier

"Go Ye to Pindo"—May 2002

"I am with you and will watch over you wherever you go" (Gen 28:15 KJV).

The sound of a braying donkey startled me awake. I reached for my flashlight. I needed light to see my clock. In total black darkness, I couldn't find the flashlight. I rose up on my elbow to reach farther. The packed straw mattress scraped the skin off my elbow. I sometimes awake in the night and wonder where I am. This night, there was no doubt. I was in Pindo in the jungle of Peru.

It was not an easy road to Pindo. There has only been a dirt road across the mountain for less than a year. We (Ken, Alex, Jose and I) traveled first by bus for 7½ hours. At the end of the bus route, we rode in a pickup truck for 4½ hours. The mountains, jungle, and people along the way made it a beautiful journey.

Pindo has always been home to Alex. Most of his family still lives there. Alex left the jungle to work in Reque. There he heard the Word of God and committed his life to Christ. He wanted to go back to Pindo and share the good news of the gospel with his family and friends.

Alex, Ken Biron, and a pastor went on that first important mission. Alex's parents, brother, sister, and other family members and friends received Christ.

The father of Alex came to the jungle at age fourteen. As he said, "Looking for a better life." He helped clear land, plant coffee, build a school, and help other settlers as they arrived. He married and to this union was born eight children.

When asked if many foreigners had visited Pindo, he said, "Only one European, right after World War II, but he didn't stay long."

Is it not time that we answer the Master's call—"Go ye to Pindo."

As dusk settled over Pindo, people began to gather for an outdoor service. There is no electricity; so one lantern was brought out to provide light. Three benches and a few chairs were placed in a circle providing seating for some. The light shone on the faces in the inner circle. Those in the outer circle stood like shadows in the night. Those who, so recently, had heard the "old, old story, that we have loved so long,"[4] sang, prayed, worshipped, and gladly received the words we shared.

They have a lot on which to construct a church. They build with adobe brick. We look forward to taking the first group of work camp missionaries to Pindo in July.

When it was time to return to Reque, the pickup truck came for us. Coffee, rice, bananas, oranges, and chickens were loaded on the truck. The twenty-eight people climbed on and the next adventure began. Perhaps later I will tell you the rest of the story.

For now, may we all be found faithful.
Roma Lee

4. "Victory in Jesus." Lyrics by Eugene Bartlett Sr.

Holidays 2002 *(Report from the July 2002 work camp)*

A Place Called Pindo *(Located in the jungle several hundred miles north of Lima, Peru)*

You won't find Pindo by accident. You must be seeking to find it. You will know when you find it—it is at the end of the road. There has been a road to Pindo for only a few months. It is still a project under construction.

A request was made for God's Word to be taken to Pindo. A pastor, a missionary, and a man born in Pindo were the first team to go. Soon, I joined the missionary, Ken Biron, for another adventure. We were the first and second North Americans ever in Pindo (God must have had a sense of humor to send us).

The people were kind and gracious. A family provided a place to sleep and food for us. A crowd gathered outside in the evening to hear Ken and I give our testimonies for the Lord. Plans were made for me to return in July with a group of North Americans.

A group of fifteen North Americans were soon ready for the challenge of a rough trip into the jungle. Each work camper was aware that they were the first group to embark on such a mission. Whatever example we were as Christians and North Americans, would be their opinion of both.

The journey began with our initial departure from our homes to Miami, and then on to Lima. We rode on a bus for eleven hours from Lima to Reque. We rested overnight and then rode a bus for seven and one-half hours from Reque to Jaen. From Jaen to Pindo, we rode on a truck for six and one-half hours. The trip from Jaen to Pindo should have been only four and one-half hours, but rain had made travel on the mountain roads slow and hazardous. Did anyone complain? NO! The mountains echoed with singing and laughter (and prayers) of work campers.

There were many highlights of our experience in Pindo...

- There was work and play with nationals.
- Cooking meals over campfires.
- Daily devotions and sharing times with our group.
- Bible school with the children.
- Sharing time with the women. Thirteen women received Christ.
- Outdoor services each evening by the light of the stars and our lanterns, with approximately 136 attending each evening.
- The sweet sound of singing, praying, and God's Word.

Yes, it is a long way to Pindo. But I was just thinking about the journey some wise men took a long time ago. They were seeking the Christ Child. They traveled until they found Him. There are many in our world today who do not know where or how the Savior may be found. This is why we continue to go and share the story of Jesus and His love. For hearts who will receive Him, Christ still enters in.

In my heart and in His heart,
You are loved!
Roma Lee

Christmas 2004

We Have Seen his Glory

"And ye, beneath life's crushing load, whose forms are bending low, who toil along the climbing way with painful steps and slow, look now! For glad and golden hours come swiftly on the wing. O rest beside the weary road, and hear the angels sing!"[5]

Grandma is small and frail. She has straight grey hair, wrinkled face and eyes that smile. She lives with her daughter and grandchildren. I always feel welcome in their little house with block walls, dirt floors, and one small window. Meals are cooked over an open fire. There are few furnishings in the kitchen—just a few old bent pots and pans. Against one wall is a pile of brush and sticks to be used for cooking the rice and carrots. My heart was sad to see that the family must sleep on lumps and piles of bundled-up rags.

When I arrived, Grandma was sitting on the side of a cot-type bed. Her bare, cold, and wounded feet were hanging toward the floor. The large toe on her right foot is missing. Her left foot was wrapped in dirty rags. Her daughter explained that Grandma had stepped on a nail and her foot had become infected. I was not prepared to take care of her need that day, but I promised Grandma I would be back with medicine, bandages, and slippers.

On the next visit, I washed her feet, cleansed the wound, applied ointment and a bandage. A work camper put soft pink slippers on her feet. Grandma was delighted and clapped her hands with joy. She asked me to pray. As I prayed, she loudly and fervently joined in the prayer. God's presence filled the room and our hearts.

5. "It Came Upon a Midnight Clear." Lyrics by Edmund H. Sears.

Also on that day, new bunk beds and mattresses were delivered (and blankets on the next visit). When we left Grandma's house, we did not go empty handed. We were given a bag of carrots. God always blesses the gift and the giver. It doesn't matter if the gift is a bag of carrots or a pair of pink slippers.

We remember the Greatest Gift ever given was not in a beautiful package but wrapped in swaddling clothes.

"The Word became flesh and made his dwelling among us. We have seen his glory" (John 1:14).

Wishing You Joy and Love,
Roma Lee

April 2009—Peru

God Will Not Forget the Love You Have Shown Hebrews 6:10

Driving down a winding dirt road, we could see signs of poverty on every side. Someone other than the ones who till the soil owned the small houses. A man with oxen was plowing a small field. Men and women wearing large straw hats were harvesting potatoes. We could almost feel the pain in their backs as they were bending low to the ground.

We stopped to visit in the home of Edison and Elena. They live in a small tenant house. Edison was not home. He was working in a sugar cane field. Their two children; Rause, 4, and Jake, 7, were at school. Both children attend the R.L.C. School (Roma Lee Courvisier School). Elena walks with the children to and from school. It is a thirty-minute walk each way.

The family is often hungry. Elena told us there have been times when all they had to eat was a bowl of rice. The bowl of rice had to last two or three days. The children would only get a small dip of rice each day. Elena is most grateful for the food the children are now receiving at school. For breakfast, the children receive a sandwich, oatmeal, and a drink. Lunch usually consists of a generous serving of rice, a vegetable, and a piece of boiled chicken or duck. They receive very large servings. Their plates are full.

Last year, there were no available funds to feed the children. Now, because of your giving, the children are fed.

I must also tell you about Betty. Betty has cancer. She is a woman with strong faith and determination. She has a fifteen-year-old daughter who will graduate from R.L.C. School next year. In spite of her own needs, Betty is always visiting, praying, and encouraging others. She is a willing helper when needed at the school or church.

Last year, when there were no funds to feed the children at school, Betty was at the school when a little girl came to her and asked, "Can you give me something to eat? I am so hungry. We don't have any food."

Betty explained that they no longer had food at school. The little girl kept pleading, "I am so hungry. Can't you give me a piece of bread?"

Betty found bread for her. The bread was from her hand, His hand, and your hand. "In their hunger you gave them bread" (Nehemiah 9:15). "Because of your great compassion you did not abandon them in the desert" (Nehemiah 9:19). God is good!

With a Grateful Heart,
Roma Lee

The Miracle—Summer 2009

Have you seen or experienced a miracle?

Some people say, "I have never seen a miracle."

Others say, "I don't believe in miracles."

It is still much the same as when Jesus walked on earth. He healed the blind, the lepers, and the crippled. He raised the dead, turned the water into wine, and fed the 5,000 and so much more. Some believed and some did not. Miracles do still happen. Sometimes Jesus lets us be part of the miracle.

I want to tell you a story about a real place and real people. It is about a place called Milagro. The English translation for Milagro is "miracle." Milagro is a community in the barren desert not far from Reque, Peru. The wind blows every day whipping the sand in faces and across the narrow roads.

Milagro is a growing community, with many humble houses for the very poor. Until recently, the most noticeable thing missing was a church.

Milagro was a community without a witness for Christ. Then Christians from the church at the R.L.C. (Roma Lee Courvisier School) found a home where they could have Sunday school. Two years ago, land was donated for a church to be built. Terrance Volden raised the first money to begin work on the church. For two summers, we have had work campers working in Milagro. There are walls for the church; the classrooms have dirt floors; and the roof over the classrooms is made from straw mats. Nearly 100 children and 10–15 adults meet there each Sunday.

Most people in Milagro still live in spiritual darkness. They are in an area known for cults, witchcraft, and gangs. Traveling down the winding dirt roads, you see the poverty, sadness on faces, and children in dirty ragged clothes. You feel the spiritual darkness and the physical hunger.

It was our desire to reach out to these people. Perhaps, if we gave them physical food, would their hearts be open to spiritual food? Jesus fed the multitude. He blessed the loaves and fish and gave them physical food. Then He taught them. In Milagro, the invitation went out, "Come and eat with us."

Preparation was made for their coming. Work campers, with shovels and wheelbarrows hauled dirt to level the ground inside the outer walls of the church. Chairs and benches were brought; a stove and huge cooking pots were hauled on a truck. A sound system was borrowed. A generator was rented. (There is no electricity in Milagro.) Women from the R.L.C. School and church worked all day preparing the food.

As darkness came, we peered into the darkness wondering, "Will they come?"

Prayers were rising from our hearts. Two mothers and a baby were the first to come. Then came children, parents, and grandparents. They were welcomed with outstretched arms, a prayer and a devotional on "Jesus, the Bread of Life." Christians from the school and church, along with work campers, served the food. Approximately 350 were fed.

The Spirit of the Lord filled the place. His presence was so real I could almost see Jesus as He moved among the people and gently touched each one.

Someone commented to me that outside in the darkness, there was a heaviness, an eerie feeling; but inside the church walls was a feeling of peace and protection. It was a feeling unlike any other. We sat with the least of these and they touched our lives.

I will be going back to Peru, September 17–27. We want to continue to build on what God is doing in Milagro. We believe more lives will be touched on a follow-up visit. We will be feeding many other families. The cost of everything in Peru has risen 18% this year. Most of the people in the desert do farm work. Farm work is seasonal. When there is no work, there is little or no food. The little food that they have has to be carefully rationed to have a small portion for the children each day. Thanks to all of you who have been part of the Milagro miracle.

I have a promise for you—right from the heart and Word of God. Isaiah 58:10–11: "If you spend yourselves in behalf of the hungry and satisfy the needs of the oppressed, then your light will rise in the darkness, and your night will become like the noonday. The LORD will guide you always; he will satisfy your needs in a sun-scorched land and will strengthen your frame. You will be like a well-watered garden, like a spring whose waters never fail."

Thanks to all of you who have spent yourselves in behalf of those who are hungry and oppressed. Blessings and love to you.

Roma Lee

Holidays 2009

Wishing you blessings—
Thanksgiving, Christmas and the New Year.
"I was hungry and you gave me something to eat."
Matthew 25:35

Milton was a strong, healthy man until one Sunday night after church when he had a stroke. For a long time, it seemed as though Milton was not going to live. Work campers visited him, prayed, and brought food for his family. It was months before Milton recovered enough to be able to walk or work. His wife Hilda worked at anything she could find to provide food for the family.

Once again, in recent weeks, Milton has barely been able to walk. Hilda faithfully cares for him, praying constantly for the needs of her family. The October food distribution was an answer to her prayers. With tears of joy, Hilda gave this testimony.

After receiving the food, their young son said, "See, Mommy, we didn't need money. God sent us food."

Thanks to all of you who gave to help provide food for this family and others.

Many of you have been waiting for an update on Milagro. Since our last report, they have continued to have about eighty-five children and fifteen adults in Sunday school. The recent food distribution in Milagro included sixty families. The average number per family would probably be five. Each family received a large box of food staples, plus two large cakes from the school bakery and a generous supply of toothpaste and soap.

Until this time, there had not been any regular service at Milagro, except Sunday school. When families received their boxes of food, they were told there would be a Bible study on Thursday night. Since they do not have electricity, lanterns are their source of light. More than one hundred came for Bible study. That is not all of the good news. More than one hundred eighty-five came for Sunday school!

I was amazed at each food distribution with how well everything was handled. The sorting, packing, and giving. Lines were orderly. No one was trying to be first. Each family signed in. If they couldn't write their name, they gave a thumbprint.

God has continued to provide funds for the children at the R.L.C. School (Roma Lee Courvisier School) to receive breakfast and lunch each day. Also because of your giving, five Sunday schools now receive a light breakfast each Sunday morning.

There is so much more. I cannot begin to tell you all that God is doing. However, I must tell you about New Reque. Some of the poorest of the poor live in New Reque. For ten years, young adults have taught Sunday school in whatever room was available. They have had to move from place to place. Most rooms will only hold about twenty-five children. Furnishings are makeshift tables, boards across blocks for benches, and uneven dirt floors—but still they come to hear the stories of Jesus.

A special day of celebration was planned for New Reque. That day arrived and what an exciting day it was! Since early morning, excited children had been jumping up and down, clapping hands, running in and out of doorways, and checking on their friends. Christians from the main church and school were hauling large cooking pots, a stove, chairs, and all things needed for this special day. Soon the large pots were filled with rice, vegetables, and chicken to feed several hundred people.

Under the canopy shelter, there was music, singing, games, skits, bags of treats, and balloons. After hearing a Bible story, the children were told, "Go get your parents. Now there will be a service for adults and we will all eat together." The parents came and listened to words from the Bible. They were attentive and respectful.

Their joy was evident as large plates of food were given to everyone. More than five hundred were fed. My attention was especially on the children.

I kept thinking, "These are the forgotten children of the world."

Then I thought, "No, they are not the forgotten. They are the ones that few people know they even exist."

Now, we know them. I know them. You know them, too. These children represent the millions of children at home and around the world who need our love and care. May we never forget them.

Roma Lee

March 2010 *(Excerpts)*

You have been a refuge for the poor, a refuge for the needy...a shelter from the storm" (Isaiah 25:4).

I returned from Peru, South America, a few days ago. I want to share some of the things God is doing here.

Many of you sponsor a child (or children) at the R.L.C. (Roma Lee Courvisier) School. Your children are doing well. It was wonderful to see their smiles, hear their laughter, and get lots of hugs. The feeding program makes a difference for the students and staff. When children are hungry and malnourished, it is difficult for them to study and learn. At school, they receive a light breakfast and a large lunch. Lunch consists of rice, a vegetable, and meat. For many, this is probably the only food they receive each day. 216 children are enrolled in the school this year, and there are 9 men and 9 women on the teaching staff. The cost for the school feeding program is $2,400 per month. With rising costs, it could cost more to continue. Thanks to you who give to feed the children.

Also, through the feeding program, boxes of food staples are given to many families. For some, it has been survival. Included in the boxes of food are rice, beans, peas, lentils, oatmeal, spaghetti, tomato sauce, tuna, oil, milk, and a large jar of jelly. The cost is approximately $60.00 for each box.

On Saturday, we delivered food boxes to the children and mothers in the community of Cusupe. Mothers, grandmothers, and children met us to receive their food. Any men who might have helped were working in the fields. The last child waiting for her food was Claudia. Claudia lives on a road where we could drive, so Ken said we could take her home. Claudia is so small, she could not have carried the food without help.

I wish you could know Claudia. She is a small eleven-year-old girl. Besides being hungry for physical food, I think she has a deep spiritual hunger. She walks a little more than two miles to Sunday school. Her seven-year-old brother, Edgar, walks with her. The two miles plus is a long walk for children, but there is more—Claudia carries her thirteen-month-old sister, Bridget, in her arms. Can you imagine how Claudia's small arms and legs must hurt after she walks more than four miles round trip on Sundays?

Last October, a Sunday morning breakfast feeding was started. This program is for five Sunday schools in nearby communities. This was to be on a temporary basis, i.e., as necessary funds came in. Thus far, the Sunday school breakfast program continues. All breakfast foods are prepared in the church kitchen located on the school's campus. A team of men and women meet to prepare the food at 5:00 a.m. on Sunday mornings. The breakfast menus vary somewhat. Oatmeal seems to be a staple. Sandwiches may be jelly, egg, or meat (either chicken or duck). A healthy drink such as a soymilk is also served.

I joined the breakfast cooks to see them in action. Some were slicing bread, others putting jelly on the bread, and another stirring oatmeal.

I asked, "How many are you prepared to feed today?"

The answer: "Six hundred."

Attendance in the Sunday schools is 450, but they must be prepared for more. No food is wasted. As food is prepared, a man from Reque comes on his motorcycle pulling a small wagon. He loads up the food and delivers it to the Sunday schools. This program costs about $500.00 a month. God is at work caring for His children, won't you join Him?

I want to thank all of you who have given to the Peru Feeding Program. You have helped Claudia and hundreds more. They are all needy. They all have a story.

Beth Moore once said, "Your tenure on earth will be incomplete without engaging with God across the globe. Find out what on earth God is doing—and join Him."

Blessings and love to all,
Roma Lee

Christmas 2010

O Come Let Us Adore Him
"I have come that you may have life."
John 10:10
"Blessed is the person that trusteth in the Lord, and whose hope the Lord is."
Jeremiah 17:1 (KJV)

Rejoice, the Lord has come! He has given hope.

I returned from Peru on November 13. While there, I saw poverty, sickness, hunger and needs of every kind. However, that was not all I saw. I saw hope in the eyes of the R.L.C. (Roma Lee Courvisier School) children, teachers, and pastors.

I saw hope in Mery's eyes as food was delivered to her. Mery lives in the midst of poverty—real poverty! She knows sorrow. Mery's husband died from lung cancer, and her daughter was hit and killed by a truck as she was walking home. Recently, Mery almost died when she had hernia surgery. She is better but still has much pain and weakness. Mery has two sons. During our visit to Mery's home, her fifteen-year-old was in another room doing the family laundry by hand. He is still in school. She also has a seventeen-year-old son. This son was out working. He has an old motorcycle taxi. In the area between Reque and Milagro, there are many moto taxis. It doesn't cost much for a ride, so a driver doesn't make much money. Her son works from 5:00 a.m. until 11:00 p.m. Mery said, "If he earns enough, we eat. If not, we don't eat."

Mery attends the Milagro church. It was there she heard the gospel and accepted the Lord. During this time of illness, some of the families in the church, poor as they are, have shared their food with Mery and her sons. Each Sunday morning, there is breakfast at the church. Because Christ came, there is a church and a feeding program. Because He came, there is hope for all of us, now and eternally.

I pray that this will be the best Christmas ever for you and your family. I do thank you for the love you have already shown in helping to feed hundreds of children and families.

I love you and hold you in my heart,
Roma Lee

A Side Trip

Colegio EFATA School for the Deaf

Roma Lee's ministry took her many times to the school for the deaf in Lima, Peru. She became aware of the school through her daughter, Lynette. This article written by Lynette shares the beginnings of that ministry.

"As I Reflect Back" by Lynette Courvisier (1985)

There she was, an adorable little four-year-old girl, on the campus of a school for the deaf in Lima, Peru. Seeing her there was the culmination of my reasons for being in the center of South America.

College is currently my main vocation. My major is Manual Communications—interpreting for the deaf. I will graduate in June of 1986.

The past quarter, I have enjoyed my practicum class intern assignment at a public elementary school where approximately 36 deaf children attend. It only took one hug from a cute little blonde headed boy in the first grade and I fell in love with the assignment.

My greatest highlight of the year was an opportunity I had to travel to South America on two different trips with my best friend—my sweet li'l mom.

Mother led a work camp to Peru in March of 1985 to build a pastor's home. Less than two weeks before we left, I was studying in my room, looking through my files, when I just happened to come across an old article I had long ago forgotten. The word *Peru* in the subtitle caught my eye. After making a closer observation, I discovered the article entitled "A Reason for Hope." It was about Colegio EFATA, a school for the deaf in Lima, Peru—the very city to which Mom's work campers were going.

Two weeks later, I was bouncing along a bumpy, dusty road in a station wagon driven by a Nazarene missionary who knew where the school was located and generously offered to drive me there. Miles and miles of poverty lined the road, homes constructed of nothing more than straw mats. In the Lima area, it had not rained for twenty-five years, so there was a mountain of solid dirt with no vegetation, which surrounded the city. Everything was dry, dirty, and very dusty.

As we approached the school, we could see a tall, solid fence, which surrounded the compound. As we drove up to the gate, a young deaf boy opened it. Entering the compound we could see a sharp contrast. Inside, I could see beautiful trees, neatly trimmed grass, and colorful tropical flowers. From the foundation to the rooftop, every classroom, dormitory, etc., was neat, orderly and literally sparkling clean.

Tagging along on our tour of the campus was an adorable little four-year-old girl who had just herself arrived at the school. (She was one of the few children on campus during the summer vacation period.) Her parents, not knowing sign language, were unable to communicate with her, so they sent her to Colegio EFATA. She was not able to sign, for no one had ever taught her the art of signing communication. This lovely little girl had no way to communicate with her parents, her teachers, the children, or me. She watched our every movement but could neither understand nor respond to what we were saying/signing.

Most children begin life with the ability to hear; therefore, learning a language comes so naturally to them. As a matter of fact, most children are able to learn about 5,000 words by the time they are four years old.

Helen Keller once said, "Deafness is the worst misfortune because of the loss of the most vital stimulus, the sound of the voice that brings language, that sets thoughts astir, and helps us in the intellectual company of man."

All morning, I kept signing to her, "You're cute," and she would just shyly smile and try to mimic my signs. To me, the absence of language and communication in this little angel's life was an even greater poverty than the meager mat homes or indigent living conditions I had just observed on the ride out to the school.

In addition to standard academic courses, the students, from the youngest to the oldest, are learning very important spiritual lessons, evidenced by the beautiful chapel on campus. The students receive an allowance for tasks they perform around the school, such as cleaning and gardening. Out of their allowances, they are taught to tithe ten percent to God, and the majority of the cost of the chapel was funded from the students' tithes. Truly, Colegio EFATA is "A Reason for Hope," for dear Peruvians!

September brought about an opportunity for me to return to Peru. This time the entire group of work campers was able to visit the school with me. I was so excited! Finally, Mother would be able to see the place I had been talking about almost constantly for six months! Ninety-five children now filled the campus, so we immediately began with a visit to the classrooms.

Kindergarten was our first stop. The moment I stepped into the room, I saw her—the same little four-year-old girl I had met last March. "Good Morning! Good Morning!" she excitedly began signing over and over. I was ecstatic as I watched her. I could see the tremendous progress she had made in the six short months of schooling. She had learned a lot of sign language, enough so that she was able to communicate with her little classmates and the teachers. She is now constantly surrounded with loving communication.

Later that morning, all classes were dismissed for a special service with our group. I had the privilege of signing a song for the children. As I looked into the face of my special little friend, tears of joy filled my eyes, for I realized that through her new found language, she is not only learning to communicate, read, and write, but she is also learning about Jesus. It is the prayer of my heart that the song I signed, "Behold God Is My Salvation," written by Allanson Brown, will soon be her testimony!

The mission trips were more than just highlights of 1985—they have been life-changing events for me.

A Side Trip

In 1998, youth and adults from the Breiel Boulevard Church of God in Middletown, Ohio, went with Roma Lee on a work camp to Lima Peru. The following is an excerpt from an interview conducted by Iona Asher with Youth Pastor, David Colp and printed in the *Middletown Journal.*[6]
"Youth Minister's work camp trip to Peru proves both a cultural and visual shock."

David Colp, youth minister at the Breiel Boulevard Church of God, thought he knew about poverty and Third World countries.

That was before he and thirty-six other Church of God members, twenty-nine of them from the Breiel Church, went to Peru on a mission venture June 5–15.

6. Reprinted with permission.

"It was far worse than I had imagined," says Colp, whose previous trips out of the country had been to tourist and vacation spots.

"Instead of the colors we're used to in the United States, everything was brown…like a desert," Colp says, remembering his bus ride from the airport to Lima.

"Absolutely nothing grows there unless someone waters it. Trash was everywhere."

"Many of the poor people live on the mountainsides in thatched or cement block homes with no roofs, no electrical power and no sewage systems," Colp says. "The higher up the mountain, the poorer the living conditions."

"It was a real culture shock for most of the group," says Colp, who was housed with the other men in his group in an unused apartment building. The women stayed in the homes of a church member in Lima and her neighbor.

The work camp team ministered to children through Sunday school programs that included clown acts, puppets, games and gifts.

Members got a real taste of how the poorest of the poor live when they climbed a steep, winding path to a small church built years earlier by work campers led by Middletonian, Roma Lee Courvisier, who also arranged for the Breiel Church trip in June.

"She has been leading work camp groups for over thirty years," Colp says. "She knew all the people who lived on the mountain (on the way to the church), and they would come out and great her and embrace her. Her impact has been felt by so many people in that area."

In addition to visiting churches and satellite Sunday schools, Colp and his companions did some painting, plumbing and electrical work at a deaf school in Lima. They conducted training seminars for the Peruvian Church of God leaders.

They also visited a leper colony where they met Hernan who only had one leg and was confined to a primitive wheelchair.

"His chair had a wooden seat, no back or footrests and no bar or pads," says Colp. Roma Lee, who had visited him earlier in the trip, told the group about his wheelchair. We took up a collection from the group members. She found a wheelchair for $250.00. We delivered it to Herman the next day.

Through an interpreter, Courvisier told the grateful leper that the wheelchair was "a gift from God." After counseling and prayer, Hernan prayed to accept Christ, says Colp.

"The trip to Peru totally changed my perspective," says Colp. "It makes you appreciate what you have and how unimportant it is," he concludes.

A Side Trip

The Roma Lee Courvisier School in Reque, Peru

Roma Lee's influence on the life and ministry of Ken Biron continues to have an enormous impact for the Kingdom. Ken tells the story of the miraculous beginning of the Roma Lee Courvisier School in Reque, Peru, and its continued influence on the desert community.

In 1990, Ken stayed in Lima, Peru, after a work camp with Roma Lee. He had little money, did not speak Spanish, and had no formal training. He was involved in the Latin American Children's Fund, a child sponsorship program. The program not only recruited people to sponsor children but had a program to assist mothers to go back to school. This program helped mothers of the children and some prostitutes leave the streets. From his first days in Lima, the Lord placed a burden on Ken's heart to start a school.

The Lord gave a covenant to Ken. God spoke, "You find the property and I will provide the money. The property must be given to you free of charge."

Ken searched in the Lima area for five years for the property. He walked throughout the city of almost twenty-one million people looking at any empty lot and even garbage dumps for the land. Everyone wanted money for the land.

Ken married Maria in 1993. In 1995, Maria's Uncle Marino invited Ken to visit the many locations of open land in Chiclayo. Chiclayo is located in a warm, desert region, 478 miles from Lima and 8 miles from the Pacific Ocean. It has only a few inches of rain annually.

Ken spent a week with Mariano looking for land throughout the small villages in the region. He needed five acres for the school, but again, everyone wanted money for the land. When asking for a donation of land, he was denied at each location.

On Friday, Ken decided he would return to the States. He went to Reque, a town south of Chiclayo on Saturday morning. He saw the mayor of the town walking through the village. It was unusual for the mayor to be working on a Saturday. Ken approached him with the request for five acres of land. The mayor stated that he would consider Ken's request. Ken returned to Lima and received word a month later that his request for free land was approved.

Ken returned to Reque. He and a local pastor then traveled to the site of the land on a motorcycle taxi. They drove past farmhouses, desert sand dunes, and trash dumps with flies and scorpions. They saw nothing but dirt and sand.

Ken thought, "Without families living in the area, where would the children come from to attend the school?"

Ken believed Joshua 1:3,5: "I will give you every place where you set your foot, as I promised Moses...No one will be able to stand up against you all the days of your life. As I was with Moses, so I will be with you; I will never leave you nor forsake you."

Ken prayed, "Lord, we have permission from the mayor and we thank you for the souls and the families that will be here."

Ken began the journey to raise $30,000 with his return to the United States. He visited the First Church of God in St. Louis, Missouri. A number of young couples were interested in a work camp to begin construction. Ken called four other churches, but none of them had money available for the school.

A week before he was scheduled to return to Peru, he met with a man who owned a youth ranch in Arkansas. At one point, the ranch owner had told a friend of Ken's that he had a burden to help start a school in Latin America and would give $10,000 to someone who could procure the land. Ken went to the meeting with great anticipation. The rancher did not recall making the statement about giving $10,000, but he gave Ken $1,000. Ken was grateful for the money, but in reality, he needed much more than $1,000 to build the school. Maria asked Ken what he was going to go.

Ken replied, "I will buy shovels and we can dig in the dirt until God provides the rest of the money."

On Saturday evening, Ken got a phone call from Mr. and Mrs. Smith (name changed to protect anonymity) requesting a meeting with Ken and Maria to discuss sponsoring children. During the evening long meeting, Ken tried discussing the need for funding of the school. The Smiths were only interested in child sponsorship.

The next day, Ken got a message that the Smiths wanted to meet again. Ken felt that there was nothing left he could share about child sponsorship. However, Ken and Maria spent the evening with the couple. The conversation once again centered around the Latin American Children's Fund projects: child sponsorship, the breakfast program, mothers' back-to-school program, and the emergency medical fund, which was used for surgery or major medical needs of the children.

As the meeting came to an end, Mr. Smith went to his desk to write a check. He gave Ken five envelopes. Ken assumed the envelopes contained checks to sponsor children.

Ken opened the envelopes when he got into his car. The first envelope contained a check to sponsor a child for two years. The next envelope contained a $1,200 check for the emergency fund. Likewise, two other envelopes contained checks in the amount of $1,200 for the breakfast fund and $1,600 for the women's back to school program.

As Ken opened the fifth envelope he stated, "Maria, they also gave $260 for the school, no it's $2,600 for the school, wait it's $26,000 for the school!" The Smiths had known Ken and Maria for less than twenty-four hours and gave substantially to the ministry of the school.

As the Birons were leaving the second meeting, Mrs. Smith said, "I am going to talk to my father about the school. If he calls you, drop everything you are doing and respond to his call."

In fact, Mrs. Smith's father called Ken and generously gave $5,000 a year for several years.

Not only did these individuals respond to the needs of the school, but also Ken called the four churches again who had previously said they did not have funds available. They each gave $1,000 each before Ken left the States for Peru. God had provided the $30,000 needed to build the school.

With great anticipation and excitement, Ken returned to Peru ready to build the school. When he and a local pastor visited the property to do preliminary work before construction, a crowd of angry peasants in pickup trucks with machetes met him. They were screaming insults because the mayor had given away land that did not belong to him. A policeman calmed the crowd, but the reality became apparent—no one was permitted to build on this land.

Jose Vega, one of the crowd, stood up and apologized for the behavior of the men. He shared with Ken that he knew a school would be positive for the community. He offered to go with Ken some other day to look for available land.

Ken stated, "When Jose took me to a piece of property, we went past the property the mayor had given us, well into the desert. I thought it looked like the end of the world. Together, we walked off five acres of land and agreed to the land deal with a bottle of soda. In 1998, we signed the official papers. The free land for the school was ours!"

The school needed a well. The lowest part of the land was across the street from a Habitat for Humanity housing development. It seemed logical that the school would be located near the development. The well drillers hit rock very quickly. The water was brackish, not potable, and sustainable for only about forty-five minutes a day. All water would need to be boiled before use. A school with an anticipated enrollment of one hundred or more children needed a better well. Ken Biron was aware of the Living Water ministry founded by Ken Buoy. Ken attempted to contact Ken Buoy numerous times. In the days before e-mail and cell phones, communication was difficult at best and the school desperately needed a good well.

Ken Biron was in the Chiclayo airport when the Holy Spirit spoke to him, "That man is Ken Buoy; go talk to him about the well." Ken obeyed the prompting of the Holy Spirit. Not only was the man Ken Buoy, but he went to the land with his divining rods. The water was at the top of the property, not where the first well was drilled. The new well was a 240-foot well on an aquifer with no need for filters.

Every school in Peru has a number or is named for a person. Ken stated, "I knew it would be the Roma Lee Courvisier School, but she was not Peruvian. If a school is named for a person, he or she must have contributed to the welfare or security of the nation. I knew she had done that with all of the work camps she brought to Peru to improve the lives of the people. The government approved the name."

The name of the school was kept a secret from Roma Lee until she visited after the school was built. Ken knew that Roma Lee would not want the attention of a school named after her. For the dedication, the name of the school was covered, but as she entered the school compound, the children were lined up shouting, "Welcome to your school, the Roma Lee Courvisier School."

There is also a church named for Roma Lee. The sign above the door in Via Milagro says "Church of God Roma Lee." The sign painters made an error and thought Roma Lee's name was part of the church name. Ken decided that since the spirit of Roma Lee's compassion for people was exemplified in the church, he would not tell anyone that the sign should have just read "Church of God."

Top: Roma Lee with a child from the RLC school.
Bottom: Playing volleyball with the youth of Lima, Peru. Pastor Willie Baraybar is on the left.

Top: Banner for the RLC school in Reque.
Bottom: Visiting with children of the RLC school.

Top: Transportation in Pindo, Peru.
Middle: First graduation class of the Roma Lee Courvisier school in Reque, Peru. 2010
Bottom: A visit to the Police Academy in Reque, Peru.

Top: Roma Lee with the old man in Reque, Peru.
Middle: Work campers making their way to Pindo.
Bottom: Roma Lee with Hernan at the leper colony in Lima, Peru.

Top: Roma Lee with children on the mountain community of Caja de Agua.
Middle: Cooking over an open fire in the jungle community of Pindo.
Bottom: Visiting with children in straw mat houses.

CHAPTER 10

Here, There and Everywhere

In Her Own Words

Early in Roma Lee's ministry, she visited many countries as reflected in the stories from newsletters. The earliest stories of miracles and God's faithfulness continue to be clear memories for those who traveled with her. The impact for the Kingdom will not be known this side of eternity.

Some newsletters incorporated reports from several countries. These newsletters give an insight in to the breadth of the ministry. She has taken groups as large as fifty-one work campers as well as trips with just one or two.

September 9, 1982

Dear Partners in Missions,

As we remember your faithfulness to the Lord and to us, our hearts overflow with love and gratitude.

We thank the Lord for His faithfulness to us. God has answered prayer again and again. He has blessed in services, given us good health, and protected us as we have traveled many miles across the U.S. and in other countries. He has provided for our needs through many of you.

One of the special blessings we have experienced recently was that of leading an Eye Witness crusade to Latin America in July. There were eighteen crusade team members representing nine states and eleven churches. We visited churches and other ministries in Costa Rica, Panama, San Blas Islands, Colombia, and Ecuador.

A new experience for most team members was that of staying in homes with national families in Costa Rica. Except for two Spanish teachers in our group, most of us spoke little or no Spanish. This was not as much of a problem as you might imagine. We found that the language of love is very effective in communication. Also, smiles and hugs are the same in every language.

We spent four nights in homes with national families. In every heart and with every family, there developed such strong bonds of love and friendship that our lives will forever be richer. The families who were our hosts treated us as if we were royalty. One lady, who kept four of our group in her home, said it was like four angels had come to visit her. None of the families in whose homes we stayed were so wealthy as to own an automobile. We walked to and from the homes where we stayed. Morning and evening, our rented bus came for us at the church in Grecia to take us to services and other activities in various places.

Since my family sponsors an Agape child (Rosaura Espinoza Rodriguez) in Costa Rica, we asked if we might stay in her home. Since they live four miles from the church in Grecia, the Lopezes (our national leaders) felt it would be better if we stayed closer to the church and in a more central location where our group could reach us. However, we learned that Rosaura and her brother Marlon had been marking off the days on the calendar awaiting our arrival and expecting us to stay with them. We knew that we must stay at least one night in their home.

Our first three nights in Costa Rica were spent with a wonderful Christian family that we learned to love so very much. In the early morning, they walked with us to our bus. One evening, they walked to the church in another community to be with us for the service. They had four beautiful little girls. The oldest child, Patricia, was nine years old. She helped me with Spanish, and I helped her with English.

The highlight of blessings in Costa Rica was to meet with a new congregation of people just starting a church in the village of Altos de Peralta. They had no church building, no property on which to build, and no funds to buy property. The service was held on the porch of a home. The yard in front of the house was filled with people. The people came from every direction. They were standing on the hillside and in the road above the yard. Others were standing somewhere in the darkness and shadows listening to the gospel. There was yet another unseen person standing in the shadows beside them. I am sure they felt His presence. One day, they will see Him clearly and love Him, too. Pray for this new congregation of people. Pray that soon they will have a church building.

One day, we visited the capital city of San Jose, which is about twenty miles from Grecia. We took Rosaura and Marlon with us. Marlon, who is nine years old, had only been to San Jose once before. I am sure that Rosaura had never been. Can you imagine the excitement of these children when taken to a museum and then to McDonald's for lunch! Later that day, we took the children shopping in Grecia. That evening we went to church in Meson near their home. After the service, we walked the dusty, rocky road home with Rosaura and her family. Their house was small, furnishings simple, a cement slab on the back porch for washing, no indoor bath, a small wood-burning stove for cooking, and a small corner cupboard for dishes. Everything, including the wood floors, was spotless clean. How blessed to be in this home, for we were welcomed and loved! We all sang hymns together—they sang in Spanish and we sang in English. Then, while Rosaura's mother prepared hot chocolate for us, we played with the children. Baby Frank (guess whose namesake he is) had lots of laughs playing with the ball and balloons.

The next morning, Rosaura's father was up at 4:00 a.m. preparing to leave for work in the sugar cane fields. He works six days a week for $10.00 a week. Before leaving, we were served a breakfast of black beans and rice. Much of our luggage was left in Costa Rica. We had packed with this in mind. But more than our luggage was left—a part of our hearts remained there also.

I knew, *"Adios y que Dios les bendiga,"* would be hard to say (Good-bye and may God bless you), but I didn't mean to cry!

A visit to the San Blas Islands, as someone in our group said, "was like walking into the pages of *National Geographic.*" The Kuna Indians are some of the most delightful and interesting people in the world. We ate with the Indians; worshipped with them; visited the Bible Institute, which is the training center for young pastors; and most of our group slept in hammocks in the home of the pastor.

In Panama, we were blessed as we worshipped with the people. We visited some old friends, made some new friends, and got a V.I.P. tour of the Panama Canal locks.

In Bogota, Colombia, Frank preached the dedication sermon for the church in the Catalina community. The church was built by work campers. In another community, we met on the site of property that we trust will be given to the Church of God for the building of a church and a Christian school. Our group, along with Brother Mendoza Taylor, joined hands and hearts as we claimed the property for the Lord and dedicated it for His work.

In Quito, Ecuador, we visited the broadcasting station of HCJB, which blankets 85% of the world with the gospel. The call letters HCJB means Heralding Christ Jesus' Blessings. For many years, our *Christian Brotherhood Hour* has been broadcast to five hundred million people over HCJB. Even before we had a *Christian Brotherhood Hour* Spanish program, HCJB took our English broadcast and translated it into Spanish at their own expense for many years.

It was a thrill to see the transmitters sending the gospel to Russia and around the world. Someone once said, "It is possible to build walls around countries, but one cannot put roofs over them."

Many people behind the Iron Curtain are being reached for Christ through the broadcasts. HCJB is much more than a radio ministry. Their medical ministry includes hospitals in Quito and the jungle areas. Also, a medical caravan makes regular trips into the jungle. They have outreach ministries in local evangelism, TV, rural health care, Bible correspondence courses, teaching, school for children of missionaries, printing, and many other programs. People of almost every profession make up the HCJB staff of more than three hundred missionaries. There are about the same number of national people on staff.

As we traveled from country to country, God moved upon our hearts. Our hearts were inspired, broken, and challenged. None of us can ever be the same as before. But, we have only just begun to see all the wonderful things that God is going to do in and through the lives of those where were on the trip. Already, some team members have helped meet urgent needs they saw.

One person in our group said that in the past she had some negative feelings about missions. She had joined us on the trip because she wanted to see for herself what missions was all about.

With a radiant smile, she said, "I guess you could say in my life, MISSION ACCOMPLISHED FOR MISSIONS!"

There is much too much concerning our trip and our total ministry to share in this letter.

Do continue to pray for us.

Our Love and Prayers for You All,
Frank and Roma Lee

Holiday Greetings 1989

It is only October, but it is beginning to look a lot like Christmas! What a beautiful scene I view outside my window. It looks like a winter wonderland. The ground, the fence across the way, the trees, and my window ledge are covered with snow. It is not yet daybreak, so the streetlights and shadows add to the beauty. There is a fire burning in the fireplace and a candle on the table—what a perfect time for us to have a visit.

It is very quiet in this early morning hour except for the ticking of the clock. As the pendulum swings back and forth, I am reminded of how precious time is and how quickly it passes. With the passing of time, God's love and the love of family and friends have become more precious to me. I want you to know that I am so thankful that you have touched my life.

How can I say thanks? There are no words to fully express the gratitude of my heart. It is because you have loved, prayed, supported, and worked with me that I have been able to continue working in the mission fields of Latin America.

Let me share with you a few highlights of work camp experiences…

First, I must say that glory and praise for all that is done belongs to the Lord. Credit for work done goes to a great host of dedicated workers who have given their skills, time, and money to minister unto the least of these, who are also some of the greatest of these. We have learned so much and received so much love. Always, when I am there in some far distant place, I think of you—when I climb a mountain, walk a dusty road, hold a child in my arms, weep with a mother who weeps, or place a Bible in an outstretched hand; I know that I am not just doing what the Lord has called me to do, but I am there in your stead, also. I feel very thankful for you and very close to you. Also, I think of you who donate thousands of dollars worth of medicine and vitamins, buy Bibles, give money for emergency medical needs, or feed hungry children. Those who go and those who send are all a part of the team.

Because of you, there is a little girl in Peru who is now healthy. For the first time in her life, she can run and play with other children because heart surgery was provided for her. The mother cried when she thanked the work campers, but Jesus smiled. At least 5,000 people in Lima, Peru, have received medical treatment this year from loving hands of work camp doctors, nurses, and their assistants.

In Naranjo, Costa Rica, a pastor and family no longer have to live in a small, crowded room in the church, because work campers built a new home for them. And just for fun, the work camp ladies took the pastor's wife and daughter on a little shopping spree. Never had the pastor's wife had such lovely lingerie and the teenage daughter, who had only one, much-too-small, school uniform, could hardly believe she was getting two new outfits for school. We also bought two new skillets to replace the old burned-up one without a handle.

Early in the year, a home was built for a family in the San Jose community of Lima, Peru. This family of nine had been living in a one-room straw mat house. Even though this family often has need of food, they gave their only possession, the land in front of their house, as the building site for a church in San Jose. In July, many work campers put their hands and hearts into the work of building a church. A dedication service was held at the close of the work camp.

In Santiago, Guatemala, a village where you feel as if you have stepped back in time and history, work campers began work on a kitchen for the church. While some dug into the earth to lay a foundation, others mixed cement. The medical team was busy checking and treating patients. A different experience for the medical team was working with conversations in three languages—the Indian dialect to Spanish and Spanish to English. Other workers had Bible school for the children each day. Two of us led a pastors' conference for forty pastors, and some worked preparing food. That is a glimpse of a day in the life of work campers!

In Matamoros, Mexico, a large room was added to the pastor's home. The pastor, his wife, and six children had been living in a house so small that it was necessary for one of the children to sleep in an old, broken-down car. What smiles and tears of joy this pastor and wife had as the building was completed, curtains hung, and two rocking chairs presented to the family. A clinic was held in the church, and all who came received medical help, vitamins, a Bible, and clothing. There were special activities for the children outside under a tree. Dr. Gilbert Wagoner had a goal of leading at least one person to accept Christ each day. The first two patients on the first day of the clinic were a husband and wife; they both accepted Christ.

You have been a part of all of this and so much more. God bless you.

On November 24, I will be leaving with a group of forty for Lima, Peru. We will divide into three teams. One team will be working at the children's home and school for the deaf. We will be doing repair work on housing there. We are planning a Christmas party for all of the children and staff. There are 100+ children in the home. The medical team will first have a clinic for the children, and then they will have clinics in other areas. A building team will be working in the community of Huascar.

Pray for our mission to Peru. The needs have never been greater. The people have never suffered more. The country is in a difficult time both economically and politically. Some of you may wonder if you can send clothes and gifts with us. I have to tell you that our luggage space is filled to capacity. However, you may send gifts of money to help. If you wish to send Christmas cards and letters, I will be happy to deliver your mail for you.

Next year, I plan to return to all the countries where we have worked this year, plus I have added a couple of new ventures to my schedule. I will return from Peru on December 8. On December 28, I leave for Antigua, Guatemala to attend language school (Centro Linguistico Maya). I will be there until February 1.

Please know that my love and prayers are with you always. I wish for you a most blessed holiday season—*Thanksgiving*, *Christmas*, and *New Year's*!

"And the Word was made flesh and dwelt among us, and we beheld his glory, the glory as of the only begotten of the Father, full of grace and truth" (John 1:14 KJV).

Behold His Glory!
Roma Lee

Holiday Greetings 1993

Mission updates from Peru, Guatemala, Nicaragua, Panama, San Blas Islands, Chile and Ecuador.

Thanksgiving, Christmas, and the beginning of a New Year.

A time to remember, to celebrate, to give thanks for all God's gifts, and to anticipate new beginnings and new opportunities.

I love this season of the year. My heart can hardly contain the joy, the love, the blessing of family, friends, and the church. Oh, the wonder of it all! The wonder of celebration and praise. The joy of remembering and giving thanks for each of you who have touched and blessed my life.

When I wrote to you last Christmas, I had just returned from Peru. I told about celebrating Christmas in a lepers' colony. As I write you now, I have just returned (only three days ago) from Peru.

Since most of you who will receive this letter are a vital part of the work that I do, I would like to share with you some of the highlights of 1993.

I began the year by going to Antigua, Guatemala, to attend language school for eight weeks. I believe my Spanish did slightly improve during this time. This was partly due to study, but perhaps mostly because I spent the majority of my time with people who only spoke Spanish. I loved being in the homes of the Indian people. They were so gracious, accepted me and made me part of their family. I felt completely at home in little houses with cornstalk walls and smoke-filled rooms where black beans and tortillas were being cooked over open fires.

It was during this time in Guatemala that I met Patricia Morgan, a sweet girl from Jamaica. Patricia had come to Antigua to study Spanish because she felt the Lord had called her to be a missionary. She was alone with almost no money ($10.00) in a foreign land. Patricia was born with a disfigured face. Then later a tumor on her head and behind her left eye had grown until her left eye had been pushed from its socket. Surgery had been only partially successful. All the years as Patricia grew up, she suffered ridicule and rejection from those around her. Even her father was ashamed of her and rejected her.

Patricia wanted to work in Guatemala with the organization, Youth with a Mission. She did not have the $75.00 a month that staff members are required to pay for room and food. Because I have been so blessed to have you sponsor me in missions, I, in turn, have sponsored Patricia this year so that she has been able to work with Youth with a Mission. We really are all workers together.

I returned again in May with medical and building teams to Nicaragua. The building team continued work on the addition to the clinic in Managua. The medical team treated about 250 patients a day in various villages.

From Nicaragua, I went to Panama. What a privilege to work on the mainland and visit churches on three of the San Blas Islands.

In June, I returned to Peru to the deaf children, to the families on Caja de Agua, and to share again the beautiful story of Jesus and His love with the lepers.

In July and August, I spent more than a month in Ecuador. Different work camp teams came in for different projects. Work was continued on the church in Quito and on the Bible Institute. A church was built and dedicated in the mountains. Construction was begun on a church in Zaballa. This project will be completed in August 1994.

In September, we took a medical team to Guatemala. We worked in two Indian villages. The very efficient, caring medical team ministered to many needy people. The country and the Indian people are very colorful and beautiful. Someone commented, "This is like walking through the pages of *National Geographic.*" We also held clinics in two communities that had recently been through the devastation of floods.

This month, I have just returned from Chile and Peru. I was greatly blessed as I delivered beautiful Christmas stockings filled with toys, candy, gum, toothpaste, toothbrushes, soap, shampoo, etc., to more than 100 deaf children and to the school staff. More than sixty-five people in the lepers' colony also received Christmas stockings, gifts, and food. Many national families received food and gifts. All of this was possible because of you who are faithful to sacrifice and serve in many ways in many places.

May we all be found faithful,
Roma Lee

A Side Trip

Iron Curtain

The *Iron Curtain* symbolized the ideological conflict and physical boundary dividing Europe into two separate areas from the end of World War II in 1945 until the end of the Cold War in 1991. The term symbolized efforts by the Soviet Union to block itself and its central European allies from open contact with the west and non-communist areas. On the East side of the Iron Curtain were the countries that were connected to or influenced by the former Soviet Union.

Physically, the Iron Curtain took the form of border defenses between the countries of Europe in the middle of the continent. The most notable border was marked by the Berlin Wall. Some places were highly guarded such as Checkpoint Charlie; however, in some places, the border was nothing more than a chain-link fence.[1]

---

1. Wikipedia.com, s.v. "Iron Curtain," http://en.wikipedia.org/wiki/Iron_Curtain. Used by permission under Creative Commons Attribution-ShareAlike License.

CHAPTER 11

My Thoughts about Roma Lee and Work Camps

As I sifted through photos from the two ten-day work camps I have experienced with Roma Lee (Ecuador in 1997 and Peru in 1998), the variety of experiences was amazing. Only Roma Lee could pack spiritual, cultural, and humorous experiences into such a short time frame. I'd like to list just a few:

- Picking stones out of beans before they were cooked for dinner.
- Painting with brightly colored latex paint on wall after wall at the school for the deaf, being careful to take frequent breaks because of the strong fumes.
- Visiting the Otavalo Indian market nestled in the mountains of Ecuador, where the tiny, short Otavalo lady ran from booth to booth asking one merchant after another in a very loud voice, "Exie, Exie, L (XXL)?" trying to find a woven vest in the size that this North American wanted as a souvenir.
- Group time, always with devotions followed with a fun time with the group to follow. Roma Lee was usually up to some trick to get the group to laugh.

- Teaching a conference to pastors from Latin countries with the help of our interpreter, Willie Baraybar.
- Teaching Bible school with children eager to hear about Jesus.
- Listening to Latinos worship our almighty God with emotion and music that included pan flutes, drums, guitars, and chullus (pronounced chew-use)—rattles made from goat hooves.
- Eating the Ecuadorian delicacy, guinea pig, at a church where poinsettias grow three feet tall, eucalyptus trees are plentiful, and turkeys roam the property.
- Standing in both hemispheres at the Middle of the World in Ecuador (0° latitude).
- Seeing people live in straw mat houses.
- Learning enough sign language to play parachute games with deaf children and hearing them laugh.
- Taking T-shirts to the leper colony, where the people crowded into a small room to listen to North Americans sing and Peruvians share in prose.
- Doing puppet shows with a sheet for the backdrop for the puppets.
- Dressed as a clown to tell the story of Jesus to children.
- Visiting the beautiful gilded cathedrals in Lima.
- Buying treasures in open-air markets.
- Walking through neighborhoods with sewage trenches deep enough for children to fall into.
- Helping to tell the story of Noah's ark in a small crowded room of a house where the smell of raw sewage made it seem like we surely must be on the ark.
- Standing on the rooftop of a building, looking over a city with piles and piles of cement blocks and rocks because there is always another level to be added to a building.

- Watching the youth of Peru and the youth of Ohio play a volleyball game as if it was an Olympic challenge.
- Climbing the steep, craggy, mountain path to Caja de Agua to hear an old lady sing praises to God. Roma Lee was wearing a back brace but kept saying to the group, "I just have to climb the mountain; I want to hear her sing."
- Remembering Roma Lee taking my husband to the airport in Ecuador to meet another group member. He ended up dancing with the Latin ladies who were welcoming a government official. Roma Lee probably didn't prompt him to dance in the middle of the airport, but she certainly didn't discourage him! She told the work camp in the morning that they passed Eric "from woman to woman in the airport!"
- Watching Roma Lee share her passion for the needy of the world through actions, finances, and devotion to those God has called her to minister unto.
- Shedding many tears as I left precious people I had known only for ten days.

— Bonnie Newell

CHAPTER 12

The Next Generation

This chapter includes writings of people who have been influenced by the ministry of Roma Lee Courvisier. The purpose of the chapter is to encourage all to follow God's leading in whatever ministry He chooses to place you. Roma Lee's ministry touched the lives of people from all walks of life and many countries. She permitted God to use her as a willing vessel to share the gospel.

Roma Lee's family has seen firsthand her willingness to follow where God leads. The impact of her life upon her family members extends beyond her trips to share Jesus with the poor in other countries. She is known to the family by a variety of names such as Mom, MiMi, Mee Mee, and Meems. They understand the importance of her work in other countries; however, the impact most felt is her ability to live a missions lifestyle in her everyday life, which include relationships with those closest to her, her family.

Lynette Grout
Daughter

"Just keep saying the name of Jesus out loud because at the name of Jesus, the devil has to flee." These were the words my mom would tell me when I had frequent, terrifying nightmares growing up and ran to her bedside for comfort. Returning to bed and hiding under the covers in fear, I would begin to say the name of Jesus aloud over and over. "Jesus, Jesus, Jesus…" Without fail, every single time I said, "Jesus," more and more peace would fill my heart and calm me until I fell back to sleep, resting in the name of Jesus. This is one of my favorite memories about Mom, because she taught me the power of the name of Jesus and it changed my life!!

The name of Jesus is what my mom's life is all about. Jesus is the focus of everything Mom does. Whether she is doing something serious or fun, her desire is to glorify Jesus. Mom has spent her life serving Jesus and leading others to Him.

Mom was very intentional about making Jesus the center of our home as she was raising my sisters and me. Every day began with scriptures, devotions, and prayer around our breakfast table. Written scriptures also filled our home, including a wooden cross with Psalm 118:24: "This is the day the Lord has made; we will rejoice and be glad in it" (NKJV).

On the dining room table there were wooden boxes filled with little scripture cards for memorization, and, of course, I never had to search the house to find a Bible. They were on shelves, tables, nightstands, and desks throughout the house. At the end of every day, our family would gather again for family devotions and prayer, usually including a story from *Egermeier's*

Bible Storybook, and a chapter from a missionary-themed book, e.g., *The Savage My Kinsman* by Elisabeth Elliott. Then as we were getting into bed, our parents would put a big stack of gospel records on the hi-fi record player that sat in the hallway between our bedrooms so the last thing our ears would hear at night were the praises of God being sung.

One of my very favorite weeks of the year as a child was the missions convention at our church. Mom virtually lived at the church for weeks before the convention preparing for it. My memories of Mom as she worked at church from dawn until dusk, day in and day out, are hearing her sheer happiness, excitement, and lots of laughter; there was never one remark about being tired or about all she had to do. Mom and her friend Olive Alexander would decorate the entire fellowship hall wall-to-wall with brightly colored booths created for every ministry our church supported—locally, nationally and abroad. They filled each booth with so many pictures, stories, musical instruments, and artifacts, it felt like you were traveling around the world. Mom's leadership and hard work made every missions convention a fun and exciting time of spiritual growth for everyone in the church, young and old!

Acts 1:8 (KJV) says: "And ye shall be my witnesses both in Jerusalem, and in all Judaea, and in Samaria, and unto the uttermost part of the earth." Mom has joyfully lived out this scripture every day of her life, whether she was

- visiting sick people in hospitals and nursing homes;
- inviting people into her home for a meal, popcorn, and Dr. Pepper;
- walking around local neighborhoods, knocking on doors, passing out candy to children, and inviting them to church;

- inviting herself into bars and brothels to love outcasts of society;
- leading Sunday school programs, children's church programs, bus ministries, vacation Bible schools, youth programs, missions conventions, and mission trips;
- traveling to ministries and places of need in the U.S. to give her love and support; or
- taking groups of people from all walks of life in the U.S. to the poorest, most desperate places in the far corners of the world to share God's love and the gospel through meeting the needs of hurting people, whether physical, medical, food, clothing, housing, etc.

Picking up Mom at the airport when she arrived home from a missions trip was one of my favorite times to spend with her. On the car ride home, Mom's whole face would light up and she would hardly take a breath as she excitedly told about all the things God had done, the people God had brought into their lives to minister to, the life-changing impacts their experiences had on all involved, and all the plans she had for the next trip.

I picked up Mom at the airport upon her return from mission trips many times a year for many decades, and every single time, Mom was as excited and fired up as if it had been her very first mission trip.

Mom has lived every season of her life with great joy, enthusiasm, and thanksgiving.

For Mom, the season of physically serving on mission fields locally, nationally, and abroad was not an easy season to bring to a close. The church members, work campers, missionaries, and nationals she served alongside became her extended family. I have seen tears run down her cheeks as she reminisces about her loved ones in various parts of the world and how much she misses them.

However, Mom has not just passively entered her next season of ministry. Her current ministry headquarters are in her living room. With great fervor, she ministers and shares God's love to others through her handwritten cards, letters, gifts, and personal phone calls.

Mom meticulously keeps up with the care and progress of friends across town, across the country, and across the world who are going through physical, emotional, and spiritual trials. In addition to her cards, letters, and phone calls, she often encourages hurting friends by sending them devotional books that she has spent hours writing personal notes in for each day's devotion. I am continually blessed and inspired by Mom's passion for her newest ministry when I, frequently, take stacks of correspondence and packages to the post office for her. Mom continues to minister, witness, build relationships, and lead others to Jesus from her chair in her living room with her heart overflowing in thanksgiving to God.

Mom is the definition of C. S. Lewis's quote, "You are never too old to set another goal or to dream another dream."

I love my mom, and my heart is overflowing with thanksgiving to God for her!

Jeannette Grout
Granddaughter

I have always been so proud of Mimi. Ever since I was really young, I loved when Mimi came to church with us, because she was famous. Everyone knew her and loved her, and I wanted everyone to know that was *my* Mimi. When I went on my first mission trip to Peru when I was fifteen, I absolutely loved introducing myself as "la nieta de Roma Lee"—it made me feel famous by association. Back then I saw it as fame, but now I see why she is so known and loved across the world—because of her love for Jesus and her servant's heart. What better things could you be known for?

I've always loved hearing "the bubblegum story." Soon after finding Jesus when she was younger, Mimi would get past a pack of dogs by feeding them bubblegum, and then she'd go tell Bible stories to kids. Besides the cute bubblegum aspect of the story, the thing I take away from it is that Mimi was so excited after she found out about Jesus that she instantly wanted to share that joy with others. That's how she's always been—so excited to share the great news of Jesus to everyone around her and across the world. I know every believer wants to someday hear, "Well done, my good and faithful servant," and I find it so cool that there is absolutely no doubt that Mimi will hear this someday. She is a perfect example of giving everything you are for Christ. Mimi is very inspiring to me, and I hope that, like her, my identifiers will be my love for Jesus and my servant's heart. Because, as we can see from her, a life spent walking close to the Lord and inviting others to join is the greatest, most satisfying, and most joyful path. I still couldn't be more proud of *my* Mimi.

Steve Grout
Son-in-law

When I think about my mother-in-law, Roma Lee, I think about a person who has given her life for the Lord and has shared her love for the Lord with many others. These people have been in her hometown and in countries outside the United States.

She never fails to have a smile on her face, and I believe that smile gets even larger when she discusses her Lord with people who yearn for the knowledge of the Lord.

I have been so blessed to be in her life, and from the first mission trip to Peru to the other trips I took with her, I have totally enjoyed her love for God's people.

I believe she operates on the premise that the goal of life is to know God and the true reward of life is to see God. I have been so blessed to know her.

Lee Ann Courvoisier
Daughter

It is a daunting task for our family to try to share some story or memory that is powerful enough to allow those reading the words to grasp the depth of Mom's faith, love, and desire to serve her Lord and others. Thousands of people through the years have shared glimpses of what we lived every day with her. None of us take lightly the amazing privilege it has been to walk this daily journey with her and the impact she has had on our lives. Watching her walk through, not just the good times, but dark broken places, has inspired us and given us courage to believe that no matter what we face, God's grace is indeed sufficient.

Mom has this beautiful gift of bringing laughter and fun, but she also walks so close to her Father that she ushers those around her into the presence of God.

In our home, missions was not a description of ministry in another country; it was one of the core values in our home. No matter where we were, that was our mission field—sharing the love of Jesus to those God had placed around us. And it started in our community.

It was a priority for mom to take her children and grandchildren to see the needs around the world. Going on mission trips began for me while I was in high school. Hundreds of memories come flooding to my mind of seeing the needs—and watching Mom do more than see the need. She was called to action, to bring the love of Jesus in a tangible way. Her passion for the sick, broken, and lost is what motivated her to raise money; take groups to build hospitals, schools, and homes; set up clinics and walk the dirty streets to find those who had no voice and no one to care.

Mom went to Guatemala twice in her sixties to language school. She led by example, showing us not to let age, finances, fear, physical limitations, or what others think keep you from going where God is leading. She taught me that when God has called you, you can trust that He will take care of you. She walked with confidence knowing that God had called her and because of that, she let nothing stop her.

I have learned from mom

- to love deeply,
- to be fearless,
- to be bold,
- to totally trust God in all things, in all places, in all situations, and
- make no excuses—follow where God leads.

Mom has passed to her children, her grandchildren, her great-grandchildren, and to hundreds of individuals who have walked with her on this journey, a legacy of deep faith, immeasurable love, and determination that refuses to give up. No words will ever express the depth of my gratitude for the privilege of calling her Mom.

Proverbs 31(NASB)

V. 20 "She extends her hand to the poor, and she stretches out her hands to the needy.

V. 25 Strength and dignity are her clothing, and she smiles at the future.

V. 26 She opens her mouth in wisdom, and the teaching of kindness is on her tongue.

V. 27 She looks well to the ways of her household and does not eat the bread of idleness.

V. 28 Her children [and grandchildren and great-grandchildren] rise up and bless her."

Thank you, Mom, for letting us see Jesus through you!

Roma Lee Veal
Great-granddaughter, Age 6½

I was named after my Mee Mee. Mee Mee taught me that our first name, Roma, spelled backwards means "love" in Spanish: *amor*! She is my great-grandma. She is a missionary. She helps little kids in Peru and all over the world. She looks pretty. Every time I see her, she has a twinkle in her eye. She has a pretty room. She treats all kids sweetly. I feel happy that she has lived eighty-four years. Mee Mee is very special. She is the best person I have ever met. I love her very much!

Lori Veal
Granddaughter

Mee Mee is one of the most special and influential people in my life. My first memory of Mee Mee was in Mt. Sterling, Kentucky, when I was three. She would pay me a dime for each scripture verse I could memorize, and she was the one who led me to the Lord. She baptized me when I was in the tenth grade. I had the privilege of going with her on my first mission trip to Peru when I was in high school. I remember walking up the poorest mountain, Caja de Agua, almost as soon as we landed. I could not believe my eyes. I could have never imagined that such poverty existed. Shacks were houses, trash was everywhere, the smell so awful, but as Meems (that's what I call her) led our group up the mountain. People would come out of their dwellings with big grins on their faces. Running to Mee Mee, yelling "Roma Lee! Roma Lee!" All kinds of people— young, old, toddlers, teenagers—they all came running, so excited to greet Meems!

I kept thinking, "How in the world do they all know her name?" Well, I soon realized that Meems was a hero to them. She helped them, she clothed them, she fed them, and she loved them. She taught them about Jesus and the good news. She gave them hope that this world is not their home.

Through the years, I was blessed to be able to go back to Peru with Mee Mee several more times. One of my favorite memories with her is going to the leper colony. She hugged on those who were considered outcasts. She made them feel like the most loved people on earth. It was so special to get to stay at the Roma Lee Courvisier School in Reque and see her influence on every single student at that school. I loved traveling with her up the mountains of Ecuador to have church with the Indians. These people served our whole group guinea pig! Big culture shock for this gal! But Meems said to pray over whatever food and drink they served us. She said she's never gotten sick. What a life she has lived! God has had His hand on her life and her ministry. Her influence is imprinted all around the world and forever in our hearts. I'm so grateful for her godly legacy.

Chris Kurtz
Grandson

In February of 2003, I faced uncertainty. At the time, our nation was at rest, and then word came down, and I was one of those first few called to duty in Iraq. The monthlong training period had certainly provided opportunity for self-reflection. In those last few days just before the big flight, I sat and wrote a letter—a letter that I mailed to my pastor, to be shared if things didn't end so well from an earthly standpoint. There are many stories I could tell about Mee Mee, but what I wrote about her, and to her, a decade ago best expresses her influence on my life.

"In no particular order I want to say thank you to my Mee Mee. Thank you for praying with me at the age of 7, as I asked Jesus into my heart. Thank you for being the one to baptize me 10 years later. Mee Mee, I am convinced that no one loves people more than you. You are my lifelong role model and I am thankful I was raised in your family."

There are a few things to point out. The most important thing in my entire life is written in line two. Mee Mee taught me about salvation and walked me through it as a kid. Although, I was "specially" important to her, so many others all over the world share that same story. Next, not only am I convinced that no one loves people more than she does, I'm also convinced that no one who knows Mee Mee would argue against that. God placed me right there in her direct line of influence. He provided me with a living, breathing, shining example of what it means to believe, obey, and live by the Bible, following Jesus. I am so thankful.

Jackson Grout
Grandson

My most distant memories consist of Mimi living with us, so I really don't know of a life without seeing her in my daily routine. Getting the opportunity to spend every hour of every day with Roma Lee Courvisier is seen by most everybody as a luxury. I am blessed to say that this luxury is part of my daily routine. Mimi has been in every aspect of my life. In my years of sports, Mimi has always been a loyal sideline cheerleader. Musically, she has strived to keep me in music throughout my life, supporting every decision I made as to expressing myself through music. Most importantly, she has been the greatest spiritual guide for me in my walk with Christ. I have the incredible blessing to not only see her in action supporting others' spiritual lives once a month, or even once a week, but every single day. This blessing spreads ever further, as I have one of the most godly examples here on earth just a flight of stairs away. If I ever have a question about anything concerning Christianity or my spiritual journey,

I can have it answered almost immediately. Because I have never experienced life without Mimi living so close to me, I tend to underappreciate this gift. People around the world would do anything to be in the position I am with Mimi.

When I was in early grade school, I saw Mimi as a key to being the most popular person at my church. I didn't understand all that she did, but I knew that she did good things for Jesus. Whenever she was at church, the congregation, the choir, and the pastor were surrounding her. Everyone wanted to talk to the Southern Sweetheart. As I got older, I began to realize why she was so popular. She had touched everybody in that church's life directly or indirectly. Almost every person in my church had grown in his or her walk with Christ because of Mimi.

Growing up, my mom always told me to count my blessings, as there is always someone who has it worse than you. Was she ever correct! I have had the pleasure of living with *the* Roma Lee Courvisier my entire life. When I was little, my sister and I saw her as the grandma that continuously spoiled us while being the most popular person wherever we went. Now, however, I see her as a role model that has lived her life for Christ, and it has shown throughout her life. The reality of her works truly sunk in when my pastor came up to me on a mission trip just to see how my grandmother was doing. In the conversation, he told me that if he worked as hard as he could for the Lord for the rest of his life, he wouldn't be able to complete a tenth of what Mimi has done in her life. I never would have expected a person like my pastor to say anything like that to me. In all reality, he was right. Mimi has done more in her lifetime for Christ than most people would be able to do in two lifetimes. Just to think, I get to live with this woman. I am one blessed kid.

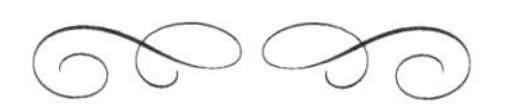

Elaine Kurtz
Daughter

How can I summarize in this short space the special moments from a lifetime of memories? Words seem so inadequate to convey what I feel about the person who has been the most influential force in my life. You may be familiar with the term *homeland missions*, but Mom's mission field literally started in the home. She tended to the physical and spiritual well-being of her family, and demonstrated by words and actions every day that same love and compassion for all those she met.

The mission trips Mom led may have had a primary focus of medical clinics or construction (churches, schools, homes) or teaching or food distribution; however, she was always looking for ways to meet urgent needs of the people she met. I have no idea how many food boxes were delivered to homes in various communities or how often money was left to help sick children receive medical treatment. The message that "God loves you!" was demonstrated through actions time and time again!

Her passion for missions was inspiring and contagious. I was continually amazed at the people who had never met Mom but who immediately wanted to be part of what she was doing. I can remember going to pick her up at the airport when she returned from a trip. I waited and watched at the gate while everyone else got off. When I finally saw Mom coming down the corridor, she was visiting with another passenger. When they walked up to me, Mom introduced me to the new friend she met on the plane who was anxious to go on a trip with her! The new friend went on multiple trips with Mom in the years that followed!

The work accomplished and the love shared on trips changed the lives of people forever, both the recipients and those whose mission was to go and to give.

One special moment that I will never forget was on my first trip to Peru with Mom. I had been on mission trips with Mom and Dad together, and with Project Partner, but this trip was the first with Mom alone leading the group. As several of us made our way along the rocky path of Caja de Agua, I remember hearing excited voices saying, "Roma Lee, Roma Lee." People came out of little thatched huts to greet her as word of her arrival spread up the mountain. Tears filled my eyes as I witnessed the hugs and love she exchanged with young and old that day. I was humbled to see how an unassuming little lady who was willing to be used by God affected the lives of people across the globe, and I was proud that this lady was my mom!

I cannot even imagine the reunion in heaven some day when the people she has touched all over the world see her again. I envision people coming from all corners of heaven excitedly saying, "Roma Lee, Roma Lee," and once again hugs and love will be exchanged in a time of great rejoicing!

Countless lives have been changed here on earth and for eternity because Mom was willing to give so others could know the love of her Savior. For the impact she has made in not only my life, but also in the lives of my children and grandchildren, I am forever grateful.

The words by Ray Boltz express the gratitude so many of us feel who have been touched by Mom's life: "Thank you for giving to the Lord. I am a life that was changed. Thank you for giving to the Lord. I am so glad you gave!"[1]

1. "Thank You." Lyrics by Ray Bolz. © 1988 by Ray Bolz.

Parishioners from the Pleasant Prairie Church of God in Satanta, Kansas shared the following thoughts about Roma Lee and Frank's ministry.

Ceil Cloud

Unconditional love for everyone is the first thing that comes to my mind. From the time the Courvisiers came to Pleasant Prairie, there was no question as to who was number 1 in Roma Lee's life. The Lord and His work have always shown through as her passion.

Whatever her hand found to do for the Lord, she always gave it her best. She made everything we did fun—VBS, youth activities, church camp, and getting ready for missions conventions. On work camps, her compassion for the lost has never been in question. She has love and compassion for people of all ages. She always encouraged us to be at our best for Him. Even when we make mistakes, there is still the godly love enveloping us to press toward the mark of the high calling of God.

It has been such a privilege to be among her friends. Even in these later years, she is still finding avenues of service to Her Lord. I thank the Lord for her example.

I would say that Sis. Co. was the glue that held things together. Her enthusiasm and passion for everything that happened at the church was awesome. Talent nights, preparing and participating in the missions conventions, VBS, Youth Quest, and church camps—all had their place in her passion of serving the Lord. Her ability to plan with making lists so things were prepared helped us all to relax and work knowing she had made preparations. She encouraged us to go and be a part of what was happening on the mission field to the uttermost. Fun and relationships were at the top of the list.

My mother and Sis. Co. were always planning the next adventure. Outreach, conventions, revivals, work camps, and always wanting to touch lives for Christ were their passion.

Only eternity will tell the lives that have been touched and changed because of her following Christ. Churches were built, bikes given, trips made, and sacrifices made. The song "Thank You for Giving to the Lord" (by Ray Boltz) tells her story.

Darla Alexander Hubbard

What a privilege it has been to have Sis. Co. there from the beginning of my life. She has been such a blessing to me. She loved me and taught me about Jesus.

She always had Smarties for the children at church. One night, Bro. Co. had a revival, and that night when I went home, I knelt at the end of my parents' bed and accepted Jesus into my heart. I was four years old.

I remember going to the Courvisiers' house one Christmas and Sis. Co.'s tree was beautiful. It had dolls from all around the world lining the bottom of the tree like a skirt. They were headed to the nativity to see the Baby Jesus. Our two families lay around the bottom of the tree and prayed. It is a special memory to me.

The Courvisiers left our church when I was seven. I was heartbroken.

When I was sixteen, Sis. Co. invited me to go on an Eye Witness Crusade to Costa Rica, Panama, and the San Blas Islands. We learned a new name for Sis. Co. Her nephew from Texas was with us the trip and she became "Ain't" Roma Lee, with a big Texas accent. We endured an earthquake, walked across the locks of the Panama Canal, and rode on the canal. The Kuna Indians were amazing.

Not only has she prayed blessings over my daughters, but she helped my mother through a tough time. Sis. Co. sent her a book of devotions for us to read every day. Sis. Co. wrote special messages in the devotional for my mother every day. What a lady!

Wanda Alexander

The Courvisiers came to Pleasant Prairie when I had been married about three years. We have many fond memories of the early years of their ministry. Sis. Co. was always actively involved as a young pastor's wife.

After we built and moved into the new church, we wanted to begin a bus ministry. We went to Hutchinson, Kansas, to pick up the buses. Sis. Co. faithfully visited the homes of children on Saturdays to invite them to ride the bus on Sundays. She started a junior church program, which continues to today. Many children were touched because of her involvement in the bus ministry.

The church had a campout each year at Scott Park. The first year, there were only two families, the Courvisiers' and ours. We built a fire and had devotions around the campfire. I slept on an air mattress, and when I woke up in the morning, I couldn't figure out why the ground became so hard. I found out that Brother Co. had let the air out of my mattress during the night.

We had Bible school each year. Sis. Co. started early, planning every detail, and as soon as it was over, she started planning for the next year. Bro. Co. led the singing and we had a wonderful time of singing and praising the Lord. The children loved both of them. Bro. Co. was a great preacher and we learned so much from his ministry. Sometimes, if he were gone, Sis. Co. would speak and we loved that. We teased him that he could be gone longer so we could hear Sis. Co. speak.

She has been the greatest example of a Christian woman in my life. If anyone asks me who influenced me the most as I learned about the Christian life, I always say it is Sis. Co.

She loves and cares for everyone. When I was going through chemo and radiation, she sent a devotional book in which she wrote an encouraging word for me to read daily. It was such a blessing and encouragement. I know she has done this for others too.

She is my faithful hero.

Phyllis O'Neal Lewis

Roma Lee is mighty special to me! I remember when she, Brother Co., and Grandpa O'Neal came to tell me that my husband had unexpectedly died at the age of thirty-seven. Our children were near the same age and we had wonderful times together. I remember Elaine and Lee Ann taking piano lessons from me. I remember Roma Lee and Brother Co. making house calls.

Steve Cloud

Keeping up with Sis. Co., both physically and spiritually, has been a thrilling challenge. Pastor Co. and Roma Lee were pastors at Pleasant Prairie Church of God when I was pastoring in central Kansas. I was only acquainted with them casually until I married Marceil Alexander in 2004. Then I began a meaningful time of seeing Sis. Co. in action. I went with her on mission's trips to Peru several times. I saw her as consistent, communicative, genuine, and fun to be with. In everything she does, she gives God the glory. In my estimation, she is a real saint!

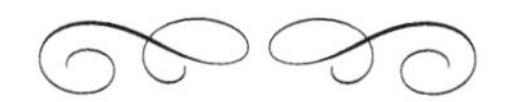

Joy Alexander Walker

Roma Lee has been such a blessing to so many people, and I am blessed to be one of them. She served the Lord in so many amazing ways. She was a dedicated wife and loving mother, and it showed through the lives of her three daughters. She allowed God to work through her, both in the United States and other countries, by actions and prayer, which go hand in hand. I still have an angel she gave me at the ninetieth church reunion of Pleasant Prairie Church. She told me to use it as a reminder that my mom was watching down on me. It has been a comfort more times than she will ever know. I am thankful my mom had Roma Lee as her best friend. I pray God's continued blessing upon Roma Lee.

John and Judy Keith
Parishioners in Mt. Sterling

Roma Lee came to the First Church of God in Mt. Sterling, Kentucky, in the fall of 1972. She was the perfect helpmate to Brother Co and the most encouraging, Spirit-filled, devoted, full-time, no-pay servant of God and of the people of First Church. As a pastor's wife, none could outwork her.

She had a great burden for children who could not get to service. In her youth, she had people that took her to church. She wanted all children to have this opportunity. She asked to start a bus ministry at First Church. Workers would visit all parts of the town on Saturday with bubble gum inviting the children to church. Many gave up their Saturdays after working all week. Many times we did not want to serve but one could not turn her down as she set the example. We worked several years on the bus routes. Many kids got to know Jesus and took the message home to their parents. The ministry started with one bus, but this proved so successful that it soon grew to four buses. The church grew so fast, we saw a need for a new facility.

In 1975, the church sold the parsonage and the Courvisiers bought their own home in Westview Estes in Mount Sterling. Sister Co. soon turned the basement into a youth center, holding Sunday school classes and fun times for the youth. You could never outgive Roma Lee. My father was ill and rushed to the hospital. She came to our home and picked up our two boys and the dog to keep with her until we returned.

In 1977, a new church was built and dedicated. This was due to the growth of the bus routes, as we were having classes in surrounding homes next to the old church. In 1978, Sis. Co. started a children's church in the new facility. Sis. Co. and her family, along with men and women of the congregation, taught children through the sixth grade. She was the first children's pastor.

Each fall during the years 1972–1980, she would be a part of a youth retreat at Glenn Eden in Beattyville, Kentucky. She served as counselor, cook, and mischief-maker to hundreds of kids from Mount Sterling, Lexington, Winchester, and Paris. All youth have many stories of Sis. Co. and Glenn Eden.

The Courvisiers had a great burden for missions. Brother and Sister Co. led the first work camp from our church to Guatemala after an earthquake in 1976. On the mission field with Brother Co., she always let him be the leader, as she was the perfect pastor's wife. She went on every work camp with all ages. She knew no stranger, no one too dirty or smelly to not need Jesus in his or her life. Her kind smile and soft words would have the grumpiest people working with her. She went on trips with youth and she was one of them.

Like Paul in 1 Corinthians 9:22–23, she became all things to all men so she might save some, for the sake of the gospel.

She truly is a remarkable woman, and our lives are changed because of her. We have followed and supported her throughout her missionary journeys.

Bob Bailey, Attorney
Greeneville, Tennessee

Where to begin! Over the twenty plus years that I have known Roma Lee Courvisier, much has happened and much accomplished for the advancement of God's kingdom, at the same time creating a close relationship that is priceless.

I first met Roma Lee through Raymond and Dereda Shelton in our church. We were anxious to develop a mission program.

Roma Lee visited early in 1989. As a result, several of us took a mission trip with her to Peru the following July.

I went to Haiti with Hand to the Plow in October 1988, which opened my eyes to the great needs of those in poverty and started a series of mission trips to various parts of the world.

Of the ten mission trips I have experienced, seven have been with Roma Lee. These trips have given me a great insight into her deep commitment of service to others.

The trip to Peru involved fifteen from our church family, along with several others. We concentrated our efforts on building a new church in San Jose, Peru, to provide for the needs of many in the Caja de Auga area of the city. We were headquartered in the Zarate Church. I recall how impressed I was with her ability to organize and keep us all focused on our purpose for being in Peru. We were able to accomplish so much for benefit of those in need.

My next trip to Peru was November 1989. We completed the church building in San Jose and worked at the deaf school and orphanage of Villa de Salvador in Efata. Pastor Ralph Shupe and I painted the dorm rooms. Steve Grout, Roma Lee's son-in-law, examined the children's eyes. Many a child ended up with Gucci glasses! It was also time for an early Christmas for the children. It was an eye-opener to see the great needs of those who could not hear and required special assistance.

My next trip to Peru, in 1990, was to add living quarters over the chapel at Colegio Efata Para Sordos, the deaf school near the Lima airport. We also built a house in Hauscar and revisited Villa de Salvador.

I recall the last evening of this trip when we were celebrating with the local folks. Roma Lee and Lynette, her daughter, did their rendition of The Judds, which brought down the house. An encore was demanded—and given, to much delight! Roma Lee was wise to make us all comfortable with the fun evening, and it did not take away from the real purpose of our trip to help those in need.

It was at the conclusion of the trip that Roma Lee was able to arrange an unforgettable side trip to Cuzco and Machu Picchu. We were visitors to this magnificent site before the great influx of tourists. She also arranged for us to have a trip to Paracas and the Ballestas Islands (seal habitat) and the Nazea Lines (geological carvings in the arid landscape).

Following the Peru trips, I traveled with Roma Lee on other mission trips. In Guatemala, we saw a country full of beauty, but unfortunately, a large part of it full of poverty and need. I can't forget the Church of the Widows in Galiler and their sacrifices, the beauty of the untouched countryside, and the profusion of orchids in bloom. We visited Lake Atitlan, Chichiastenango, Antigua, and Puerto Barrios.

Our work on this trip to Guatemala was to add a second floor educational unit to the church building in Coban. We had to cross over three mountains from Guatemala City to get to Coban. We spent five days on this project.

There is no doubt as to the most remembered trip of all. It was the bus ride from Greeneville, Tennessee, to Guatemala City. Nine of us, including Roma Lee, drove our old church bus to Guatemala, some 2,836 miles, across the southern United States to San Benito, Texas, crossing into Mexico at Matamoras (with all the problems of entry) and then crossing Mexico into Guatemala. It was a six-day trip.

I shall never forget the many adventures of this trip, starting with the bus. It was loaded down with used clothing, building supplies, and food. It had a pickup truck in tandem, which was loaded with a gas stove and refrigerator, extra gas cans, and the bus seats taken out so we could comfortably ride the trip.

Driving down the interstate in lower Alabama and Mississippi, I recall many cars driving up the side of the bus, slowing down to look at us, probably wondering just who we were.

The husband of one of the ladies told us when we left Greeneville that he would come to Knoxville (sixty miles away) to pick us up. He did not believe that the bus would make it to Guatemala! We surprised everyone as we made the entire trip without a hitch, except for the border entry problems.

During a rainstorm in Texas, we almost had a collision when a vehicle veered in front of us, but our driver was able to avoid any contact. We all believed it was our guardian angel taking care of us!

Before we sold the bus, we used it at the work location as sleeping quarters for the women in the group. The men slept in the little church. We had a temporary shower and outdoor privy.

It was remarkable the amount of work accomplished, but more remarkable was how it helped the destitute people in this community. We built a church in the Delores community at the foot of an active volcano.

The bus was finally sold and all the title and transfers made just before departing for home. We called this our mission trip of miracles!

Ecuador was the next country for mission work with Roma Lee, in 1992 and 2005. On the 1992 trip, we added a third floor to the Quito church. Adding the third floor involved a lot of steel and concrete. I shall never forget seeing the special truck required to pump the ready-mix concrete up to the third level. Many an Ecuadorian was on the ground level watching; this was probably the first time for them, as it had to be specially arranged at high cost. But it accomplished the purpose, and the third floor was completed before we left. (Ecuadorians usually transport cement to the second or third floor in a bucket using a pulley.)

We also took a side trip to work on a little church in the remote Meridiano area of Ecuador. I shall never forget the difficulty in arriving at this destitute area with almost no road for the last several miles. It created great anxiety to many in the group as we traveled in and out from the work site.

I recall this trip and the side experience, which occurred when the pastor's wife, in arranging for our sleeping quarters, thought Roma Lee was my wife and set aside our quarters! It created quite a laugh in the group!

On this trip, as in all others, Roma Lee was always careful to add side trips into the local open markets and an occasional stop for meals at quaint places with scenic beauty. This always helped us adjust our thinking and appreciation for all the many privileges we enjoy, but at the same time, it kept us sensitive to the needs surrounding us as we moved about.

In Ecuador, we passed through the Center of the World (0 degrees latitude) several times as we passed over the equator going to and from our various mission stations.

My last visit to Ecuador was in 2005, after a twelve-year absence, to help with the critical food program for the church families. I was amazed when I arrived in Quito and saw all the food that had been put together for distribution. I do not know the total cost of this food, but I do know that Roma Lee was successful in raising thousands of dollars to pay for it all. What a joy to see the faces of the wonderful folks who arrived to receive their church distribution and leave with joy in their hearts. There is no way to measure the great benefit to God's children from this program that through recent years has provided these people with their very existence.

There are two events that stand out in my mind from this trip. In addition to the food distributions, we went to the new church at Cangahua on Mt. Cayambe. We got up early and traveled by bus for some time to get there for Sunday worship and food distribution. It is an area of great need, and it was inspiring to see such Christian dedication in the people.

The other was a trip south to the Bela Vista church under the guidance of Gloria Salano. We crossed a hanging bridge over the river. The visit on the other side was well worth the trip over the bridge. Other visits on this last trip included new churches at Roldos, Zabala, and Santa Clara de Veintecatro de Julio. All churches had been started since my last trip in 1992. It is a real testimony to the work of Roma Lee and so many who have worked tirelessly to take the word of God into these communities over the years and particularly to the outstanding work of Jon and Karen Lambert, our church missionaries in Ecuador.

On this trip, I became familiar with the Children of Promise child sponsorship program. I decided to sponsor a young fellow named Freddy Calvo. I continue to sponsor him to this day. It gives me much joy to know that I can help this fellow become a contributing member of God's kingdom.

Each mission trip was designed to help in some small way with the poverty surrounding each visit, never forgetting that each act of kindness was another way of expressing God's goodness to those in need.

Thank you, Roma Lee, for being such a dedicated servant. Your crown will have many stars for your selfless giving of yourself to so many.

Donna Keith
Hamilton, Ohio

On my first trip, I remember going to a slum (Caja de Agua) on the mountain and watching the people come out of their homes in droves just to see Roma Lee. That made a powerful impression on me at the time. They loved her and cared about her. I learned later, as I grew to know her, that she loved them just as much as they loved her.

We shared many trips together and were friends but I grew to know her well after I volunteered to help her with mission accounts in the 1990s. I have always been impressed by the fact that she never loses her cool. Even in the most aggravating or tense moments, she never shows irritation or impatience.

Karen Lambert and I were teaching a sewing class in Ecuador. We taught the ladies to quilt fabric and make it into a tote bag. The touching part about this story is that they didn't think they would get to keep the totes. They were thrilled when they realized they got to keep them. The women were so touched and grateful for such a simple thing.

I have never known anyone in my entire Christian life who is more dedicated to the ministry that God gave them. Her life has revolved around this ministry. She is so gifted with people that she can "talk" them into anything. She has a way with people that makes them want to help her and be a part of her work. She could even talk the Hispanic customs workers into moving the luggage of a whole group through customs without being opened and checked. On all the trips that I have made with her, we never had our luggage searched. That is miraculous in itself.

She is the most special person I have ever met. I feel honored and blessed to have her as a friend and to have traveled with her. I can talk to her about anything, and I know she would do anything for me. I am a better person for having known her.

Bonnie Yancey

Like most people attending an evangelical church, I had seen many missionary presentations over the years, but I never imagined that I would one day be able to share some similar experiences. My interest in missions became more hands on when my husband and I were introduced to the concept of short-term mission trips in the mid-1980s.

My first overseas mission experience was with a group led by Roma Lee in 1986. We traveled to Peru and worked at one of the sites, building homes on Caja de Agua and assisting in the medical clinic in Zarate. I can recall vividly how surprised I was when I first saw the group gathered in the Miami airport—over fifty individuals so diverse in age, background and experience that I thought it an impossible task to ever expect to accomplish all that needed to be done in the short time available!

How wrong I was. Back then, I thought that "mission" was to build a house, distribute clothing, tend to the sick; but it was really so much more. How can you imagine or measure what is actually accomplished when people gather together in the name of Jesus to give of their time and talents? I don't think we can ever know the full impact made as a result of the outpouring of God's grace into the lives of individuals as they seek to enjoy fellowship together while ministering to the needs of others. That grace was manifested in the relationships formed between the work campers and with the nationals, in the experiences that will be fondly remembered and told again and again over the years, in the love shared and received by so many, and in the faith that was challenged and deepened.

I learned another valuable lesson after I returned home and began preparation for the slideshow presentation I planned to share with our church. I wanted to challenge the congregation to become more aware of the needs of others by showing slides of the poverty we experienced in Peru compared with the abundance we enjoy at home. I hoped to make my point by interspersing pictures of our local children among the slides I took of the children in Peru. I visited a nearby school and asked permission to photograph children at play during recess. I was shocked by what I observed. Many of the children I saw on the playground were just as needy and starved for attention as the church we visited in Peru. I believe the lesson the Lord was showing me was that there are people in need everywhere; we don't have to travel half way around the world to find hurting people!

My husband Tom and I each made several more mission trips over the years, and each time new friends were made and new lessons were learned; but many of the experiences were a direct result of the faithfulness and love shown by Roma Lee. Over the years, she has become an inspiration, mentor, and friend. She has demonstrated that it is possible to face life's challenges with grace and peace. Roma Lee's example and our mission experiences have led us on a continuing journey to know and share God's love with the people and in the situations He brings into our lives.

Thank you, Roma Lee, for being such a faithful servant. We love you!

Willie Baraybar, Pastor
Ventanilla, Peru

The first time I remember seeing Roma Lee was in one of the hotels in Lima. One of the workers was very excited and told his coworkers that Roma Lee had promised him a Bible. She had brought it to him that day, and he showed it very proudly.

Years later, when she started coming to Lima more frequently, I met her.

She said, "What is your name?"

I said, "Wilfredo."

She replied, "That name is too long and hard to say. Willie will be fine." She started calling me Willie. In those days, I could hardly speak English, so I didn't argue.

Through the years, her love and care for the people brought out in me the same kind of love. Her passion for evangelism, her stories about how she started knocking doors when she was just a new Christian, gave me the courage and passion to do it also.

She frequently would say, "Willie, you have a sweet spirit." One time I asked her what that meant. She explained to me that I was easy to forgive. She told me something that I couldn't see myself that built in me the intention to live that way.

After some years of discipleship, she said, "Some day, when Willie becomes a pastor, we will come and help him to build a church."

I laughed, "Roma Lee, you are funny. Me, a pastor? No, no." Now, my wife and I have been pastoring a church for thirteen years.

She has influenced my life through her personal care and love for us, her testimony of life, and her deep love for Christ. Her influence has imprinted on my family a love for Christ and for the people. I try every day to carry with me her sweet spirit and passion to serve the Lord.

When we were in the Zabala church in Quito, Ecuador, for the first time, she directed the team to proclaim in prayer, to declare that place for the Lord. We all went on our knees praying and declaring that. Years later, exactly in 1999, we did the same kind of prayer in Ventanilla. My wife and I have pastored the church in Ventanilla for thirteen years.

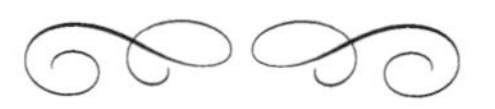

Patricia Morgan

Go Into All the World and Share the Love of Jesus

I was working as a missionary with Youth with a Mission (YWAM) in Jamaica when I felt God wanted me to go to Honduras to serve. I had never traveled by myself, and going into a country where the language, culture, and people were different was very scary for me. The director at the YWAM Honduras base suggested that I learn Spanish before going to Honduras. I was told of a school in Guatemala, so I made plans to attend the school.

I arrived in Guatemala, January 27, 1993, late in the evening, to find that there was no one to pick me up from the airport and I didn't know how to get to my destination. After and hour and a half journey in a taxi, I was at the address of the Maya Language School. It was closed for the day and now I had nowhere to go and no one I could call for assistance. The taxi driver helped me find a lodging for the night.

The next morning, I was up bright and early to proceed to find the school. I showed the address to my host and he pointed to where I should go. I found it! The director apologized for not getting the information that I was coming. He got me situated with a Spanish family who would provide me room and board. I was informed that I would pay $100 U.S. per week for room, five days of board, and four hours each day of Spanish classes.

On the weekends, the family did not provide food, so I bought bread and strawberry jam.

I was able to pay for the first two weeks of class, and then the money I had, dwindled. This was my first time leaving home and country by myself. Now I lived in a strange land. I felt there was no hope in sight.

On one particular day while on break from class, the students from various countries were out on the sidewalk to sit for a minute or two. I went out to sit and this lady came and sat beside me. She introduced herself as Roma Lee Courvisier from the United States. Immediately, we just clicked as she shared with me that she was learning Spanish to better communicate the love of Jesus. I shared with her that I was from Jamaica and I was at the school to learn Spanish to share the gospel to the people God had called me to serve. I told her I had planned to go to Honduras, but the door was just closed and I was praying to determine what to do next. She was very encouraging. As I walked in the street with Roma Lee, an indigenous Indian girl made fun of me and this just added to my pain.

The Lord sent an angel to minister to my needs, and I was given hope that He who called me would provide and make a way when there seemed to be no way. My heart was encouraged when Roma Lee reached out to me by being my friend.

After three months at the school, I left Antigua and moved to Guatemala City to join the staff of YWAM. When I left Jamaica three months prior to go into all the world and preach the gospel, I certainly did not anticipate the challenges that I had to face at the darkest moments when I felt God, family and friends had abandoned me. Roma Lee came to me in that darkest moment. I was only twenty-three years old and living in a country where black people were treated as less than human. I have faced rejection all my life and have longed to have true, genuine people in my life. Roma Lee has been a true friend who has been there for me since I met her in 1993.

I spent four years working with YWAM in Guatemala. God is so good, and if it weren't for Him, I would have lost hope. I thank him daily for his blessings on my life. At one time in my life, I thought I could never make a difference in the world and that I couldn't impact lives for the glory of God. The Lord Jesus sends people in our path that let us know we can do all things through God, who gives us strength. I thank God for Roma Lee always making mention of me in her prayers because she has a heart after God and she goes above and beyond to help those in need.

Roma Lee continues to bless me. One Christmas she sent me money and I then sent it to my family in Jamaica, because they were poor and lacking food. I thanked Roma Lee for the blessing.

Roma Lee was there for me in Guatemala, and nineteen years later she is still there for me. She continues to pray with me and sends me encouraging notes to remind me of the faithful God we serve. I haven't seen her since 1995 in Guatemala. I have had many challenges in my life, and Roma Lee and I have often talked about our health.

She would say, "Patricia, you are a strong woman." I am a strong woman because God has graced my life with Roma Lee and she cares for me with the heart and hands of Jesus.

When I was hungry, she gave me money to buy food; when I was cold, she sent me sweaters; when I was down and hurting, she comforted me. Roma Lee is a friend who has stuck closer to me than my own relatives. She is the heart of God reaching out to a hurting world.

Betty L. Barker
5 time work camper

A work camp isn't just about work. It's about a whole myriad of emotions that you're not expecting. It's giving but receiving more. It's laughter and tears. It's getting a glimpse of how people live in much of the world.

A work camp brings bonding with team members that lasts forever. It brings joy from the hugs of beautiful children and smiles of appreciation from their parents.

A work camp stretches your heartstrings until you think they will surely snap. Saying goodbye brings sadness but leaves you with memories that warm your heart. You hold your family a little closer. You look around and feel blessed with what you have but guilty because it's too much.

You remember the nudging from the Lord to leave family and country behind for a short time. You remember how you were blessed through songs with words you didn't understand. You remember the joy of the Lord on the faces of your brothers and sisters in Christ in another part of the world.

David K. Young, MPA, CEBS
David K. Young Consulting, LLC

My opportunity to go to Peru with Roma Lee began in January 2011 with a brief note on a donation check that I sent to Roma Lee for her feeding program. I had written that I might consider going with her on a future trip if there was room for me. To my surprise, Roma Lee quickly responded to my note and told my wife CynDe that she wanted me to go with her on the next trip. I didn't talk with her that day, but CynDe stated that Roma Lee felt my contacting her about going was in God's timing and for a reason. She told CynDe she felt it "completed the circle that I had asked to go with her." What she meant was my grandparents' influence in her life and her later being involved in missionary work were being completed by my going on a trip to Peru to work with her.

I didn't hear anything further from her until March 5. She called to let me know she had a trip planned in April and wanted me to go with her then. I had too much already planned in April for a ten-day trip out of the country, and thus I felt I couldn't make the trip. I thought that would be the end of it. She wouldn't hear of it and said she would see if the trip could be rearranged around May 17 with the others who were going with her. When I hung up the telephone, I felt she would not be able to adjust the plans for multiple people within a few weeks and I wouldn't hear any more about going with her in the spring. I assumed she would be going down again on another trip later in the year and I could go with her then. To my surprise, the following Thursday she called back and had rearranged the trip so I could go. I will never regret going with her on the trip; unknown to me or others, that trip would be her last mission trip out of the country. That fact became significant to Roma Lee and me later.

My grandparents took Roma Lee to church. As a result, she accepted Christ. When Roma Lee began her missionary work, our family supported her missionary work for many years.

One of the last instructions my dad gave to my mother before he passed away was, "Don't forget Roma Lee." In turn, when I began to take care of my mother's finances, I took on the responsibility of making sure money was sent to Roma Lee's work.

As a side note, on the Sunday following her call on March 5, I had a vivid dream early in the morning about being in Peru. In the dream, I was driving through some desert sand hills on a narrow paved road. At the time I had no knowledge of the terrain or environment of the Roma Lee Courvisier School location. Roma Lee said in passing not to expect to be in the beautiful part of Peru because the school was in a desert. After the dream, I got up briefly. After laying back down, just as I was drifting back to sleep, I heard in my heart, "You are called." It jolted me back awake and I lay there awhile wondering if it was just in my mind, or God speaking to my heart. I determined that I would wait to see whether it was God speaking to me or just a passing dream and a passing thought as I was going back to sleep.

In the dream about Peru, I was driving through some sand hills and parked to wait on something. I was looking out the windshield at a hill sloping upward in front of the car, and that was the last thing in the dream I remembered. The first morning I was at the R.L.C. School, I stepped out the front door of the guesthouse and to my excitement and amazement what I had seen in the dream lay before me, less any buildings (we arrived after dark the night before). Everything seemed the same; the lighting, the color of the sand, and the slope of the hill were the same, except in the dream there were no buildings and no fence around the school's property. Later in the week, I climbed up on the fence and looked at the scene outside of the fence, and it was very similar to what I had seen in the dream. I pondered all that I had seen during the week in Peru. On the last morning, I woke up with the thought on my mind, "It is not about buildings and structures, but about my people."

Please believe me. I am not making this up. what I saw in my dream and what I saw both driving to the spot where I parked in the dream and the slope in front me was what I saw in reality.

The experience had a major impact on my life. I serve on another missionary board that ministers to the poor along the Texas-Mexico border. We supply food, medical supplies, and clothing to about thirty thousand people in several locations from west of Del Rio, Texas, to Brownsville, Texas. I have been serving in that ministry since 1997, and I have traveled several times to the locations along the border. The living conditions on those locations in Mexico are very similar to what I saw while in Peru. Peru added to my experiences of helping the poor for God's kingdom and to His glory. It makes me appreciate what He has given us here in the U.S. I was emotional a good portion of the trip back home from Peru. On the plane, there was an older lady in the seat next to me reading her Bible the entire way back to Miami (almost six hours). She didn't speak English, but I think she saw me and probably wondered what was wrong with me. I wondered too if maybe she was an angel sent to be with me going home. There is nothing like living among the very poorest of our world for over a week, yet at the same time seeing the joy of the Lord in their faces too.

Roma Lee strongly encouraged me to become involved with the LACF (Latin American Children's Fund) board. As a result, I volunteered to serve on the board and will be going back to Peru in the future, Lord willing. My role on the board is partly to help with cash flow concerns and how to better improve the finances of the ministry. Having only served less than a year, I am still learning my way around the issues facing the ministry. I will forever be grateful that Roma Lee and I connected just in time for me to go with her on her last mission trip out of the country.

Roma Lee brought a picture to Peru of her daughter and me in front of her house in Texas in 1954. She gave the picture to me. She said she hadn't been looking for the picture, but rather was going through some other things in her closet when the picture fell out of a box and onto the floor in front of her. It happened just prior to her leaving for the trip to Peru. Coincidence? No, I think it was one of those "God winks" letting her and me know this was indeed the circle being completed. God had a purpose in it happening as it happened. As I like to say, time will tell if anything more is purposed other than just my going with her to Peru on her last trip.

Tom Yancey

There was a film made a few years ago called *Pay It Forward* about people repaying acts of kindness with acts of kindness to others. The legacy of the movie showed the many lives that were touched because of the actions of one person. Roma Lee has been that person in the life of my wife and me. The opportunities for short-term service have affected us as nothing else we have ever done. Even though we rarely find ourselves on mission fields these days, the experiences provided to us because of our relationship with Roma Lee lives on.

Our daughter Katherine has been to the Roma Lee School in Reque, Peru, twice. Our son Matthew has been to Costa Rica, Ecuador, Malawi, and the Dominican Republic on short-term trips and will soon be leaving for Honduras. His wife Shayla has been to Ecuador and Malawi. Bonnie's parents both were able to experience mission work firsthand in Costa Rica and Peru and later went on to work with Nailbenders for Jesus building and remodeling churches in Arkansas. With our experiences on the field, Bonnie and I have been working with the Southern Baptist disaster relief organization providing meals for the victims of natural disasters like Hurricanes Katrina, Rita, and Wilma.

In my Sunday school class, we were able to help one of our students go to China as a short-term missionary. Another student spent five months on the field in Southeast Asia working among the Muslim population.

On a trip to Lima with Roma Lee, I met a young man named Joaquin. He was from a wealthy Catholic family in Lima. Joaquin became a Christian in his early twenties. He became a pastor and felt called to minister in both the men's and women's prisons in Lima.

After meeting with Joaquin, Roma Lee approached a few of our group and stated that she felt the Lord calling some of us to go to the men's prison with Joaquin to encourage him and the prisoners. About ten of us were to go the next day.

The next morning, we met with Joaquin and boarded the first of three buses for the long trip. When we arrived at our destination, there was still a long way to walk to the remote location. Soon, I could see the barbed wire enclosing a large stone fortress-like compound with a massive solid steel door. The soldiers were everywhere carrying automatic weapons. After a few minutes of questions from the guards, we were allowed to pass the barbed wire and move toward the steel door. Against the outer wall of the prison, there were many lean-tos and straw mat huts.

"Who lives there?" I asked Joaquin.

"The families of the prisoners," he responded.

There is no social welfare system in Peru; the families camp out by the prison in hopes that their men will be released some day. In Peru, when someone is sent to prison, there is no timetable for release. The prisoner may be released tomorrow, next week, next year, or never. The families just wait and hope. I remember thinking that it is impossible for the Word to go forward in this place of no hope. Joaquin is kidding himself if he thinks that anything can make a difference here.

We approached the steel door and entered the darkness inside. We were required to empty our pockets—wallets, passports, keys, everything. We were given a numbered brass disk and told that if we lost the disk, we would not be allowed to leave.

Joaquin led us across a courtyard where men in rags, who appeared to not have had a bath in months, wandered aimlessly about. Guards with submachine guns were everywhere.

Again, I thought, "Joaquin, you are fighting an impossible battle here."

We walked down some filthy, stinking hallways, and then I heard what sounded like singing. Our group turned a corner into a bright, whitewashed room and saw at least one hundred men sitting on rough hewn benches, singing in Spanish, "When we all get to heaven, what a day of rejoicing that will be. When we all see Jesus, we'll sing and shout the victory."[2] I couldn't believe my eyes! Then, I saw, painted on the white wall, some green letters saying "Nuestras Esperanza Nueva—NO MAS MUERTE" (Our New Hope—No More Death).

There was a long Bible passage directly under this statement in Spanish—"In an instant, in the twinkling of an eye at the sound of the last trump, for the trumpet shall sound and the dead shall be raised incorruptible and we shall all be transformed. For this corruptible must put on incorruption and this mortal, immortality and when this corruptible has put on incorruption and this mortal, immortality, then shall be brought to pass the saying—Death is swallowed up in victory. O death where is thy sting? O grave, where is thy victory? For the sting of death is sin and the strength of sin is in the law but thanks be to God

2. "When We All Get to Heaven." Words by Eliza Hewitt.

who giveth us the victory through Jesus Christ our Lord" (1 Corinthians 15:52–58 KJV).

Then I saw the verse 58 and it hit me like a ton of bricks: "Therefore, my beloved brethren, be ye steadfast, immovable, always abounding in the work of the Lord for as much as ye know, your labor is not in vain in the Lord."

It was a powerful lesson handed out in an unlikely place to a surprised recipient, thanks to the faithfulness of Roma Lee and a young pastor who followed his call forward in this place of no hope.

Over the years, I have learned to pay attention when someone says, "The Lord laid on my heart to give you this to take with you to the mission field." I believe that, given past experience, if someone wanted me to take a dead elephant with me, I would try and find a way.

Many years ago, while preparing for a trip to Peru with Roma Lee, a man said that he felt I was to take a duffel bag full of upholstery material and spools of industrial thread to Lima. I had already packed my wife's sewing machine to take for the women of the church at Zarate, so I thought that the thread and material would work nicely. In many Latin countries, I knew that sewing was a very important part of the lives of the women of the various churches and I thought Peru would be the same.

Upon arriving in Lima, Salomon Cabinillas, the national church leader, said that he knew of no women who sewed anything in the area. I wondered what I was going to do with the sewing machine, material, and thread.

Days passed and the machine and material sat in a corner. Then Brother Joaquin, the prison minister, came for a visit. He brought with him some crocheted baby items made by the inmates at the women's prison in Lima. He told us that when a woman goes to prison in Peru, she has nowhere to place her children. Many of the women take their children to prison with them. The government believes that it must feed the inmates but there is no responsibility to feed the children since they are not there because of any crimes they may have committed. The women must share the little food they receive with their children in order to survive.

Brother Joaquin started taking in some yarn and patterns and the women started making small items that Joaquin tries to sell in order to buy a little extra food for the women and their children. He showed us the items and asked a very small price and hoped that maybe we would purchase a few items. Of course, every item was purchased immediately for prices much higher than what he requested.

Brother Joaquin thanked us and said that he was very excited because he saw that small stuffed animals sell very well at El Mercado Indio (The Indian Market, a large tourist market in Lima). He was able to acquire some patterns for these animals and was currently looking to see if he could find a sewing machine to take to the prison. I told him that I had brought one and would be honored if he would take it to the ladies. He was overjoyed and said that now only one thing was lacking, some very thick material and strong thread for the animal's bodies. I asked him if the material that he needed was like the type used on furniture cushions. He said that is exactly what was needed. I handed him the duffel bag of material and thread. We cannot always see the plan as it unfolds, but if we are faithful to the call, we may see the hand of God in everyday actions.

Our lives have been touched by Roma Lee's love and compassion. We have been so moved by the experiences that she allowed us to share that we have never been the same.

When I think of Roma Lee, I remember Paul's words, "But by the grace of God I am what I am, and His grace toward me was not in vain; but I labored more abundantly than they all, yet not I, but the grace of God which was with me" (1 Corinthians 15:10 NKJV).

We thank Roma Lee for all of her love and encouragement all these years. May the Lord richly bless her.

Rod Roe, Associate Pastor
Eaton Road Church of God
Hamilton, Ohio

What can one say about Roma Lee Courvisier? With her big disarming smile, she just has a way with people, whether it's coaxing the most backward and shy child from his or her shell or challenging the most stolid of customs officers in the Lima, Peru, airport who insisted that import taxes must be paid on two wheelchairs. The wheelchairs I speak of were meant for two poor souls in a leper colony on the outskirts of town whose bodies were so ravaged by the dread disease and walking was such a painful endeavor that they had become dependent on others for their mobility.

As in the parable of the widow in Luke 18, Roma Lee persisted. She was neither rude nor disrespectful, nor was she fearful. She carefully explained the intended purpose of these wheelchairs and assured him that they were a gift and no profit would be made, and besides, it was to help his own countrymen. In the end, the customs officer, wearied of this persistent woman who spoke Spanish with a Southwest drawl, told her to take the wheel chairs and go! Taxes waived.

I once asked Roma Lee which work camp was her favorite. She smiled real big and said, "Whatever one I'm on!"

I have grown to know the truth and wisdom of her response. I remember my very first work camp with Roma Lee. In 1993, a large group from the Millville Avenue Church of God in Hamilton, Ohio, went to Quito, Ecuador, to help construct a building for the new church plant in the very small village of Zabala. It was after midnight when we arrived at the Bible Institute in Comite, where we stayed during the work camp. Roma Lee, true to form, had already developed the room assignments even before we arrived.

As she called out our names and told us which floor and room we would be in, she turned to me and said, "You'll be rooming with the Peruvians."

I put on my best smile, but inwardly thought to myself, "Oh Roma Lee! You're putting me in a room with Peruvian nationals? I don't even speak English well, let alone Spanish!"

As it turned out, she had assigned me to a room with Ken Biron, Willie Baraybar, and Hector "Coco" Ararand. All three spoke English (better than I do), and all three were as much big jokers as I was. Our room may not have gotten as much sleep as the others, but ours certainly had the most fun! By the end of the week, I had discovered just what an honor and a blessing she had bestowed on me.

I have been on several work camps over the years with Roma Lee and have grown to love missions because of those trips. In fact, not only do I love to go on the work camps, I love to hear the stories of others returning from theirs. Over the years, I have heard amazing stories coming from returning work campers—miraculous stories of healings, language barriers being overcome as nationals hear preaching in their own language without an interpreter, of food being multiplied, stretched beyond physical possibility to feed a long line of Central American Indians. The stories and events inspire joy and praise to well up from the very depths of your soul!

However, there is one miraculous event in particular that will forever stand out in my mind that, in my opinion, was the most miraculous one of all. And I was there to witness it!

We were on a work camp at the school in Nuevo Reque, Peru, pastored by Ken Biron and his wife Maria. It was a Sunday afternoon, and as is tradition on our work camps, we were out visiting the various Sunday schools and home churches in the outlying villages. The last one we visited that afternoon was in a little community called Cusupe. This village is located half way between Nuevo Reque and a fair-size town called Munsefu. Cusupe is a farming community and appears deceptively pleasant. I say deceptively because, although it's located only a few miles from the Pacific Ocean, this northern part of the country is primarily coastal desert. Since Cusupe is basically made up of several large farms, there are a great number of irrigation ditches. Therefore, the area appears quite lush and green, but life is hard for the people of this village. I also say deceptively pleasant because crime is rampant in the area due to the remote location. Robbing, assaults, and rape are common in the area.

When you turn off the main road, you find yourself traveling down a long, narrow dirt road that has a constant deep layer of loose dust. The tires of the trucks and vans kick up large dust clouds behind them as you bump and bounce down the road. A mile or so down the road, you come to a path that is impassable for motor vehicles and you have to walk the remainder of the two hundred yards to the village. The village itself is just a random grouping of adobe mud-brick buildings. As you enter the village, you hear the clucking of chickens and your nostrils twinge at the familiar smell of pig (familiar, at least, to those of us who have ever visited a farm).

We gathered into an unfinished adobe building for the Sunday school service. It was unclear whether this building was someone's home or just a small meeting place, or both, which is most often the case. We all sat down on wooden benches of rough-sawn wood planks and listened while the children of the Sunday school sang songs for us. The adult teachers shared about their ministry. After prayer time, all work campers passed out small bags of candy to the children. (The adults were grateful to get some candy too.)

As we slowly exited the building, a woman came up and said that her mother had an injured ankle, was ill, and wanted Roma Lee to come pray for her. Of course, Roma Lee didn't hesitate. Off she went with this stranger, a couple of work campers in tow. We entered an adobe home just a short distance away and were led into a very small room that had a small bed frame made of rough-sawn boards and one small table. The mattress on the bed, if you could actually call it a mattress, was made up of a thin piece of foam rubber padding and covered with a cloth, probably the best bed in the house. Lying on the bed was a very frail and elderly woman. She was lying very still. Her voice was soft and quiet. Her eyes were dull and lifeless. She appeared to me as one nearing death.

Roma Lee came in and sat on the edge of the bed and spoke tenderly to this woman. In a very few minutes of talking with Roma Lee, this woman sat up on the edge of the bed. She was amused when Roma Lee told her of how as a girl she worked the cotton fields on a farm back in her home in Texas. After a little while, Roma Lee had her smiling and laughing with charm and funny stories. The woman giggled, giggled mind you, like a school girl when she found out that she and Roma Lee where the same age!

I watched as I stood there, amazed at the transformation. The old woman had come alive! She was laughing and smiling, showing all the remaining teeth she had. She seemed to regain her strength and be renewed right before us. The most striking thing to me though was looking into her eyes. When we had first entered the room, her eyes were dull and lifeless. Now they were bright, shining, and full of joy. As they sat on the bed together, they laughed and joked, and Roma Lee hugged her over and over again. The time came when we had to leave, so we gathered around the woman and prayed for her. Somehow it was a different woman sitting there as we went out the door.

Miracles. Please don't think me irreverent, but speaking in other languages—no problem for God. Healing the sick and injured—a snap of the fingers to Him; after all He designed us. Multiplying food so many are fed from a little piece of cake (pun intended). No, the most amazing miracle of all is how God can restore hope and bring renewed life. How awesome is our God! How marvelous is He! Think about just how loving He must be. God loved a little elderly woman so much that He sent a group of North Americans 3,500 miles by plane, vans, and walking to a small obscure farming community, just to tell this woman that she is loved and to give a hug to her from Him. The most amazing miracle God does is in the heart of man. How He can restore hope to the hopeless, revive those who have given up! Isn't that the greatest miracle of all, that God loves us so much that He'll pull out all stops to tell us so? Even going all the way to Calvary. How great is our God! I have a picture of Roma Lee sitting on that bed hugging our little grandma (for that is how we affectionately refer to her now). It hangs just over my bookcase of devotionals and doctrinal books. I keep it there to remind me what those books are truly about.

I can tell you that Roma Lee would never wish to receive a single compliment that she thinks belongs to the Lord. It would grieve her immensely to think that any praise would be given her instead of to our Lord. Roma Lee understands the heart of Christ. She understands what's important to Him. She reflects His grace, overlooking all offenses. She mirrors His love, reaching out to those who need Him most. I have seen her pick up and hold close children with very snotty noses and lice-infested hair, and hold them as if they were her own. She continually demonstrates just how good our God is, both in voice and actions.

What can one say about Roma Lee? Well done, good and faithful servant!

Bush Stevenson
Mt. Sterling, Kentucky

It is a joy and privilege to share with others some of the wonderful experiences I had with Sister Co.

In 1974, I was attending Mt. Sterling First Church of God, where Bro. and Sis. Co. were pastoring. She urged me into the bus ministry because I worked well with children. I was involved in children's church, so it was natural that the bus ministry would fit me. Sister Co. was my teacher as she went with me to find children to ride my bus, a new route. She had many ways to know if children lived in a house.

She would say, "Stop here."

Then she would jump out of the car and run up to the door. It was amazing how she projected the love of Jesus to those people she met for the first time. I was overwhelmed at her energy and vitality. She never tired of doing God's work.

One particular Saturday, we were looking for children from house to house when she suddenly said, "Stop!"

I stopped and she jumped out to run up to this house. There were toys and a swing set in the fenced in yard. As she started through the gate, my eye caught sight of a sign that read, "BEWARE OF THE DOG!" There was an old dog lying in the yard that seemingly would hurt no one. Out of the corner of my eye, I saw something that left me weak and speechless. Sister Co. was trotting up the walk when a large, black German shepherd headed straight for her, teeth showing, and looking aggressive. I tried to yell at her to warn her, but I couldn't make a peep, for fear had gripped my being.

Sister Co. went right up onto the porch, knocked on the door, with the big black dog jumping up and down beside her. It never even touched her.

A woman came to the door, looked at Sister Co., looked at the dog, looked back again at Sister Co, and said, "Aren't you afraid of dogs?"

Sister Co. told her that she had always been terrified of dogs but when God sent her to pick up children for the bus ministry, she asked God to take care of the dogs so she could pick up the children. God did and she did.

Sister Co. is a wonderful servant of God. She loves to laugh and have a good time. She has a heart that beats for Christ Jesus. I love her and count it a marvelous privilege to have been a worker and servant in the kingdom of God.

Jon Lambert, Missionary
Quito, Ecuador

Our lives are like tapestries created by the threads of our experiences. My name is Jon Lambert. My wife Karen and I serve as missionaries to the country of Ecuador. Into the lives of my family God introduced a new thread in 1986. We were new pastors at the Millville Avenue Church of God in Hamilton Ohio, and Roma Lee's pastors. The Lord began weaving a newer, deeper calling into the lives of my family and myself.

That same year, a humble woman in Ecuador was beginning her journey to find God. Delia Rodriguez lived in the remote Amazonian town of Lumbaqui. In those days, the only connection most people had to the outside world was by listening to a shortwave radio. On her radio, Delia listened to the Spanish version of the *Christian Brotherhood Hour* program. She wrote a letter asking where she could find a Church of God congregation in Ecuador. She had accepted Christ and wanted to learn more. There were no Church of God congregations in Ecuador in 1986. Delia started the first house church. From there, the church has grown to seventeen congregations. That house church and Delia would later become another part of our tapestry.

In 1997, Roma Lee asked me to go to Guatemala on one of her work camps. Like all pastors, I was busy and ten days in Central America did not fit into my schedule. However, who could resist the constant, loving persuasion of Roma Lee?

"It will make you a better pastor, Brother Jon," she said with that smile.

The Guatemala trip changed my life. Actually, I can honestly say that it was knowing Roma Lee that forever changed my life. Throughout the next ten years, I traveled once a year with Roma Lee on trips to Central and South America. I especially remember one trip to the Caja de Agua barrio in Lima Peru. On the first day, we climbed the dirty, narrow streets of that grey-brown, crowded place. We were going to build a house for some orphans.

Suddenly people began to shout, *"Roma Lee esta aquí, Roma Lee esta aquí!,"* which means in English, " Roma Lee is here!"

As we continued our climb, the narrow streets became lined with smiling faces. People rushed to grab her hands and embrace this humble woman. The only times I saw Roma Lee uncertain and overwhelmed was when people tried to give her praise. That, she would insist, should only go to the Lord.

In 1997, my family and I resigned as pastors to enter missionary service. The first person we told of our decision was Roma Lee. After all, it was all her fault!

We were asked to go to Ecuador. In Ecuador, we would work with many wonderful Christians, including Delia Rodriguez. Delia has started and served as pastor of seven of our seventeen congregations. I asked her once who was her mentor, who had been the greatest influence on her Christian walk.

Delia furrowed her brow and with a look of questioning astonishment said, "My dear Brother Jon, for all of us, it is our Roma Lee."

If I could tell you only one story that describes this woman of God, it would be about the famine in Meridiano. In late January 1999, we received a call from Roma Lee. She seemed troubled. She asked about our remote congregation in the village of Meridiano. We told Roma Lee that we had not received any word from Meridiano for several months. News from this little town deep in the coastal cloud forest is hard to visit in good weather. Normally, we are not able to travel to that area from December through February. Roads are often washed away by landslides caused by the winter rains. Roma Lee proceeded to tell me that the church in Meridiano was in trouble.

"They are starving, Brother Jon," she added.

Roma Lee had a dream. She told me that in her dream she saw three of the leaders from the Meridiano church pleading for help. They were asking for food and they all appeared thin and pale. Roma Lee proceeded to tell me that she could be in Ecuador by March and she would be bringing enough money to buy food for Meridiano. I had known Roma Lee long enough to know that when she says someone is hungry, they are hungry.

The first of March, we had our monthly pastor's meeting. Two of the leaders from Meridiano had managed to attend. They were thin and weary. The little valley depends on selling their tangerine crop in order to buy staples to get them through the rainy season. The rains came early that year and closed the roads earlier than usual. The crop was lost and food staples did not get delivered.

In the meeting the Meridiano leaders asked, "Can you help us? Our families are starving." At that moment a shiver went down my spine.

"My brothers," I said, "We already know. Help is on the way. Sister Roma Lee will be here later this month to buy food."

One brother, Jorge Betancourt, collapsed sobbing. Between the tears, he told us how one night in February, his family was around their kitchen table and all the children were crying from hunger.

Bro. Jorge said that he slammed his fist down on the table and looked up to heaven and yelled, "Oh God, do you not see that we are starving? Can you not send us someone to help?"

As this little frail man regained his composure, he again looked up and clasped his hands and prayed, "You did hear us Lord, forgive me, please forgive me for my doubt."

When Roma Lee arrived later that month, she brought enough funds to provide food staples for Meridiano and all our other congregations in Ecuador for well over a month. Over the next ten years, Roma Lee's food program bought more than $400,000 worth of food and thousands were fed.

Paul Jones
Church of God Career Missionary to Bolivia since January 2004

In the early 1980s, I was a young man looking for direction in my life. I had committed myself to following the Lord and sensed God's call to service, but I had no idea what that meant. Visiting with my grandmother, Louise Harrington, one Saturday put into motion the details that would start me on a rather unexpected path. As I began that morning talking with my grandmother, I merely mentioned that maybe I might want to go on a mission trip somewhere. Enough said. She immediately picked up the phone and began making calls. After contacting Roma Lee, she handed me the phone. I've always been a man of few words, but with Roma Lee's non-stop excitement, I could not get a word in edgewise. I really don't remember any of the details of that conversation but, by the time I hung up, I was enlisted for the next work camp scheduled for Lima, Peru.

The trip to Lima was indeed a life-changing event. It started in the Miami airport. While we were getting acquainted and getting checked in, Roma Lee came to where the group was sitting. With her characteristic skirmish smile, she said with a chuckle, "We've got a problem. They say we have too many suitcases. You all pray."

She went back to the ticket counter. I have no idea of the conversation that transpired, but soon all the bags were checked and we were on our way. While this was surprising to me, after several more trips with Roma Lee, I found out that problem-solving was the norm rather than the exception for her.

That trip changed my life's direction, but I hated that trip! After three days, I promised God if He would get me out of there, I'd never go back. I understand now that what I had was a severe case of culture shock. I guess I'm not good at keeping promises, because within six months, I was on another trip with Roma Lee. Her enthusiasm has always been contagious, and I came down with a strong case of it. I, too, became excited about being involved in something far greater than myself. Roma Lee's love for the people and desire to help in whatever way possible inspired me to think more about the needs of others. During the next few years, I couldn't get enough. I began going on every trip that came up, until something in me changed.

One day, as I was talking to a fellow work camper while walking the streets of Lima, Peru, a light turned on within me that revealed the direction for my life. Wanting to change the impoverished condition of the people had motivated me to travel on many trips, but suddenly I realized there was a far greater poverty than the material needs of the people. God showed me clearly that He was calling me to minister in a more direct way to help meet their spiritual needs. This would require more than I could do on short-term mission trips. I would need to study the language and live among the people and dedicate myself to full-time service. I thank God for the experiences that He granted me—work with Roma Lee, sense her enthusiasm for life and ministry, see her pass through times of adversity with a gleaming smile on her face, and be motivated by God's love flowing through her to others. Truly God has used her to open my heart and hear His call to missions.

About thirty years have passed since the Saturday morning conversation that changed the direction of my life and ministry. God has used many things to put all of the details in place, but one special person has truly played a key role in all of this. I thank God for using Roma Lee Courvisier to plant the seed of missions in my heart.

Rev. Dr. Eric Newell
Hospice Chaplain
Middletown, Ohio

In the mornings atop the then unfinished seminary building in Quito, Ecuador, I would go with coffee in hand as I looked out over the city. I could smell the aromas of open-air markets as I marveled at the many crowded, unfinished buildings in the city; but more than that, I marveled as I thought about the energetic woman, Roma Lee, whom God had burdened with the passion for the people of Latin America.

As days passed during this work camp, my marvel included the resilience of the Ecuadorians. When in the modest homes of nationals, I sensed God's hand upon the work taking place. People who had little were willing to share what they had. I saw this come to light in two distinct ways during the work camp. People in their local congregations gave of themselves, and what they had. Work campers also, a diverse group of interested individuals who had come together to experience missions, gave from their own spiritual and personal strengths. I believe God blessed both.

Personally, I realized during the work camp that not only did Roma Lee care for the many to whom she ministered in Ecuador, but she watched over the work campers.

Early in this particular work camp, a member of our group was arriving late. Roma Lee asked a couple of us if we would like to go with her to the airport. Though late, I was glad to go. When we arrived, there was much excitement! It sounded like a party! Roma Lee and Willie, a national pastor from Peru, informed us the excitement was for an Ecuadorian dignitary arriving on the plane. Waiting on the arrival of this important person, were two large groups in two circles dancing just outside the airport. Curiosity got the best of me and I moved closer and closer to see the dancing. Suddenly, I had gotten too close and was pulled into the dancing group. Before I knew it, I was given an Ecuadorian flag and I was dancing with the rest of the group. I was really glad Roma Lee and Willie were close by as they eventually rescued me from the celebration. I'm sure they could have rescued me a little sooner, but they were enjoying watching this North American dance in a not so graceful way alongside Ecuadorians!

The experience in the airport showed me a happiness and celebrative attitude of the people of Ecuador. Yet this was exceeded by joy I would see later during this trip. Over and again, I saw joy on the faces of people as they experienced the love of Sister Roma Lee Courvisier.

Sandy Decker

Memories with Roma Lee: Never sleeps, always concerned about others, loves people, loves watermelon, loves fun, bringing gifts of love, loaded down with gifts for the children, and cares deeply about the hurting, blind, crippled, and lepers.

She has a true servant's heart, true compassion, absolutely selfless, never thinking of herself or putting herself first.

The love my husband and I have for missions was born out of the Courvisiers' ministry. Brother Co. married my husband Larry and me in 1960. We were sheep in that flock for thirteen years. They brought missions into our church in a concerted way. We had a mission convention each year, bringing in different missionaries as speakers. We met many missionaries and heard many mission stories that influenced and touched our lives. We decorated booths in the fellowship hall to represent various places the church supported missionaries; it was always an exciting time and such a blessing as we worked together.

Brother Co. and Sister Co. were always a barrel of fun. They put on skits for our programs at church. She ministered right along beside him, always involved in serving. When Brother Co. was no longer able to travel, it was no surprise that she easily transitioned and continued leading mission trips. Many times she went along to pursue her love of serving and caring for the hurting.

When one goes with Roma Lee, he or she is in for a treat. There is always fun, excitement, surprises, and blessings. Not only was there laughing, but there were also tears. Roma Lee always included sightseeing side trips, shopping, etc. She knows how to include all of the things that make a well-rounded experience.

Four generations of my immediate family have had the blessing of accompanying Sister Co. on mission trips. We treasure the memories of the trips.

One situation that stands out in my memory happened on a trip to Panama in 1983. The group was traveling through the jungle on the last train of the day. Since none of us spoke Spanish, we relied heavily on our leader, Roma Lee! The train made periodic stops through the jungle, and at one such stop, Roma Lee disembarked to ask some questions. The train promptly started, leaving Roma Lee standing there in the jungle. At first, we were just panic-stricken. Her daughter Lee Ann was also on this trip. We naturally turned to her to be our leader. She immediately began to lead us in choruses such as "Not by might, not by power, but by my Spirit saith the Lord."[3] These songs began to comfort our hearts that He would care for Roma Lee and her frightened band of followers. Someone at that station offered to take her to the city of our destination. It was an angel,

3. Lyrics by Leslie Phillips.

I'm sure. We didn't even know our destination, but God took care of all of us, and later that night, we were reunited. She actually beat us to our destination. Praise God. Her nephew Scott was on this trip and we all got such a kick out of his calling her "Ain't Roma Lee" in his Southern drawl.

On the same trip, we experienced our first earthquake in Costa Rica, 5.7 on the Richter scale. The earthquake happened at night and we were all separated from each other because we were staying in various homes in the town. It was frightening at first, not being able to communicate because of the language barrier and not knowing where everyone was staying. God cared for us in a miraculous way and there were no injuries. Sister Co. knew that we were all concerned and began to immediately round up her flock. We were extremely happy to see her and each other.

On this same trip, we went to the San Blas Islands. I have never had a fear of flying, but when we got the first glimpse of the airplane that would take us to the San Blas Island, I was just a little concerned. I became more concerned after we boarded. As usual, nothing runs on time, and after waiting a long time, one plane was ready to go. It wouldn't take all of us, so Roma Lee insisted that we go ahead. We found out that the ones who stayed behind got McDonald's. What exciting and lasting memories.

All went well and we had a wonderful time. We worshipped with the Kuna Indians, slept in hammocks, bought unusual jewelry made from seeds, shells, coral, and animal teeth. We ate food that was even more unusual.

She was always the first one up and the last one to bed. You could count on that like clockwork.

My last trip with her was to the Roma Lee Courvisier School in Reque, Peru. Due to circumstances, Roma Lee's daughter and granddaughter, my grandson, and I got to the school ahead of the rest of the team. That experience set the stage for one-upping her on the best experience of the mission trip. On this trip, she had a beauty shop contest. She had the winner chosen unbeknown to the rest of us. It was a riot watching the competition where three of the boys were models and three of the girls were hairdressers. They were all such good sports, and my grandson and her granddaughter were the winners.

When I lived in Kansas, Sister Co. asked me to teach a junior girls' Sunday school class. I felt very inadequate, but she kept encouraging me, and I taught the class for many years. I am thankful that she persevered.

Thank you, Sister Co., for the memories, your example of love, faith, sacrifice, service, humble spirit, sense of humor, and courage. What a beautiful example for us to follow.

Steven Taylor

A Faithful Servant

"But God chose the foolish things of the world to shame the wise; God chose the weak things of the world to shame the strong. He chose the lowly things of this world and the despised things—and the things that are not—to nullify the things that are, so that no one may boast before him" (1 Corinthians1:27–29).

"Has not God chosen those who are poor in the eyes of the world to be rich in faith and to inherit the kingdom he promised those who love him?" (James 2:5).

The first time I met Sister Roma Lee Courvisier was at a faith promise gathering at the First Church of God in Morehead Kentucky. My pastor, Allan Hutchinson, shared a little about his mission trips with her. As I entered the sanctuary where she was interacting with some of the people in attendance, I witnessed a meek and aged lady with a glow all about her face. I don't believe I have ever seen her without a smile. I heard of some of the physical ailments she had to contend with for quite a long time and my thought was, "How can God accomplish anything great through this weak and frail woman?"

And then she began to speak!

"Commit to the Lord whatever you do, and your plans will succeed" (Proverbs 16:3). "He who is kind to the poor lends to the Lord, and he will reward him for what he has done" (Proverbs 19:17). "He who gives to the poor will lack nothing, but he who closes his eyes to them receives many curses" (Proverbs 28:27).

The Holy Spirit began to speak through her and witnessed to me of her tremendous love for Jesus Christ and her love for the body of believers, the church, no matter what color, creed, or location. She had a compassion for the people she was sharing about that could only come from God. From that moment on I knew she and I had kindred spirits.

"And if you spend yourselves in behalf of the hungry and satisfy the needs of the oppressed, then your light will rise in the darkness, and your night will become like the noonday. The Lord will guide you always; he will satisfy your needs in a sun-scorched land and will strengthen your frame. You will be like a well-watered garden, like a spring whose waters never fail" (Isaiah 58:10–11).

In Ecuador, I entered the room where the packaged food was stored. The amount of food to be loaded onto trucks and delivered to congregations was such a great amount that I had to turn sideways to get through the room. The Spirit brought to my memory the accounts of Jesus feeding the multitudes with very little. I was amazed to hear the accounts of the thousands this food drive would reach, how it would add to their faith, change lives, and draw others to Christ. I heard Sister Roma Lee sharing about a previous time where God had come to her in a vision of the people here in Ecuador starving, eating roots to stay alive. God provided a way to get food to them through her obedience and faithfulness.

"In their hunger you gave them bread…Because of your great compassion you did not abandon them" (Nehemiah 9:15, 19).

I traveled to a few of the congregations to celebrate God's provisions. I witnessed Roma Lee's love for the people everywhere we went. Two scriptures describe Roma Lee:

> "You have been a refuge for the poor, a refuge for the needy in his distress" (Isaiah 25:4).
>
> "He [God] will not forget your work and the love you have shown him as you have helped his people and continue to help them" (Hebrews 6:10).

Jennifer Morrison
Software Developer
Dallas, Texas

I was born in Guyana, South America. I came to the U.S.A. in August 1980 to attend college. I was raised in a Christian home, but it wasn't until the death of my father in 1986 that I gave serious consideration to my faith.

I was haunted by my father's words to me, "For what is a man profited if he shall gain the whole world, and lose his own soul?" (Matthew 16:26 KJV).

Sadly, it was then that I realized I was religious but did not have an intimate relationship with Christ. Thereafter, I rededicated my life to Christ and sought to really know him and live for him.

I would like to think of my meeting with Roma Lee as "when purpose meets destiny." I was on an American Airline flight in January 2000 to Marion, Indiana. I was headed there for a surprise sixteenth birthday celebration for my goddaughter. At the gate, the agent informed me that I was assigned to a seat that didn't recline. He asked if I wished to change seats, offering another window or aisle seat. I opted for the aisle that was closer to the entrance of the plane. When I got to my seat, a beautiful, elderly lady with a warm smile greeted me. As I nestled into my seat, strapping myself in, she offered me some of her snacks. I thanked her and showed her I too had some. Back in those days, the airlines offered passengers a grab bag as they boarded the flight. This was our icebreaker and the beginning of a wonderful friendship and journey.

She told me she was returning from a mission trip to Peru. When I heard the word mission, my ears automatically perked up and my mind began churning, wondering if this was a God thing. She told me she had served in local and overseas missions for more than twenty-five years. I listened in wonderment as she told me how she began in ministry as a young girl, her work with women, and working in partnership with her husband. She shared how she took work campers to various countries in Central and South America. After a while, believing it was God who placed us together, I asked if it would be okay for me to go on one of her missionary trips. She talked about other mission organizations and suggested that I may also want to consider them.

As she continued to share, she said, "You know what, I do believe this is a divine appointment and it's not by chance that we are seated together."

I told her of the changes in my seating arrangement. She promised that she'd ensure there was room for me if I wanted to go on the upcoming trip to Peru in June. She promised to send me additional information about her ministry in the mail. She encouraged me to pray, seeking God's guidance, and if I felt led to go, she would be happy to have me as part of her team. My spirit soared, for I truly believed that it was God who purposely placed her on the flight and who had my seat reassigned so His plans for me could be set in motion.

In the late 1990s, I was praying intensely and believing God for a change in a particular situation in my life. During that period of praying, I began to sense a call to missions. The church I attended at the time was a small church and not actively involved in either local or overseas missions. I wasn't clear how to proceed with what I was sensing in my spirit, but as I sat on that flight next to Roma Lee, I believed that God was about to make this a reality.

As promised, Roma Lee sent me additional information about her overseas mission. I recall listening to the tapes on my drive into work. I wept as I listened to her sharing the familiar message in a fresh way of God's love for the world and how He sent His only Son to die for our sins. She declared that each person in the mission field was a precious soul and that if they were the only ones, God would still have sent His Son to die for their sins.

I prayed about traveling with Roma Lee in June of 2000 and felt strongly led to go. That year I traveled with her to Peru and Ecuador. I traveled with her almost every year until 2007. During those times, I've helped with the building of a church at Ventanilla, Peru; participated in food and clothes drives; visited the leper colony, school for the deaf, women's shelter; visited and ministered to families in the communities; assisted in the building and other activities at the Roma Lee Courvisier School; and participated in church services and revivals.

The leper colony was one of my favorite places to visit in Peru. The colony was a segregated community and the people living there were discriminated against. Many of the family members living in the community did not have leprosy, but they endured the same treatment as those who had leprosy. The people were shunned, neglected, and treated as outcasts. Roma Lee encouraged us to touch and love on every one, even the lepers, just as Christ did. She led us by example. She shared that many longed for the human touch. During our visits, the group played soccer with the locals; gave out clothing and treat bags to the children and adults; and held church service.

We had lots of fun too on our work camps. One fun and unforgettable trip was when we traveled to the jungles of Peru in July 2002. We started our journey on a bus to Pindo. We got off the bus where the paved road ended, and then all of us (luggage and people) were miraculously packed into a small pickup truck for the next four hours. The drive was a challenge, a testimony to our dependence on God and the skills of the truck driver. The dirt roads were narrow and rough with many deep potholes along the journey. The truck often swayed, and I wondered on many occasions whether we were going to make it. Twice we got off the truck because it was stuck in the mud. We sang hymns and prayed all the way. I can't ever recall singing and praying so much on any trip.

As we traveled the narrow paths along the sides of mountains, I would glance from the truck down to the cliff and feel that deep pit in my stomach. We sang many hymns that seemed fitting for the occasion: "Leaning on the Everlasting Arms" (especially when the truck was leaning), "On Christ the Solid Rock" and "I was sinking deep in sin" (when we were literally sinking), and "I'll Fly Away" (when we thought that we may see the other side of heaven).

Besides the challenges of the journey, we had lots of laughter; we kept the faith because we had a great leader in

Roma Lee; and we quickly bonded since we were packed in closely together like sardines. The beauty and grandeur of the Andes Mountains under starlit skies also echoed our songs of "How Great Thou Art" and "Majesty." When we got to Pindo at the end of the dirt road, the locals warmly welcomed us.

God has placed several people along my path during the course of my life. As He developed my spiritual characteristics, one of the key persons to influence my worldview on missions was Roma Lee. I've learned much from her. God commanded us in Matthew 28:19-20, "Therefore go and make disciples of all nations, baptizing them in the name of the Father and of the Son and of the Holy Spirit, and teaching them to obey everything I have commanded you."

Roma Lee has demonstrated this command by living it, not only to me but also to many others. I've seen her taking the gospel to the downtrodden and outcast, love the loveless at the women's shelter, reach out with a hug to both children and adults; touch the untouchables at the leper colony, feed the hungry, and clothe the needy. She has prayed for women, sponsored children, been an advocate for children's education, and worked to improve the living condition of families. Time and time again, she has responded to the physical and spiritual needs of many families.

Her actions remind me of Jesus teaching in Matthew 25:35–36: "For I was hungry and you gave me something to eat, I was thirsty and you gave me something to drink, I was a stranger and you invited me in, I needed clothes and you clothed me, I was sick and you looked after me, I was in prison and you came to visit me."

Through Roma Lee, I became more aware of areas in my life that needed development. I've learned the importance of the human touch. I've found myself touching, hugging, and taking more time to listen to the residents at the nursing home. As a role model, she has influenced me to sponsor a child at the Roma Lee Courvisier School in Reque, contribute to food drives, and give more financially to the work of missions.

I've developed a deeper appreciation and sensitivity for missions. My heart's desire is to become a full-time missionary. I am grateful to God for allowing my path to cross with Roma Lee's. She is my spiritual mission mom. Through her, God has set into motion His purpose for me serving in full-time missions. Even though, I'm not there yet, I do believe that one day I will be. I praise God for Roma Lee, a woman of God; her work in the mission field; and the many lives she has touched, including mine. I believe the total impact of her life on earth will not be known until we are in eternity. Thank you, Roma Lee. I love you! "And if you spend yourselves in behalf of the hungry and satisfy the needs of the oppressed, then your light will rise in the darkness, and your night will become like the noonday" (Isaiah 58:10).

Ken Biron
Missionary in charge of field operations
Roma Lee Courvisier School
Reque, Peru

When I think of Roma Lee, I am reminded of Jesus and the disciples in John 1:35–46.

> John was with two of the disciples and when he saw Jesus passing by, he said, "Look, the Lamb of God." (1:35)

Phillip, like Andrew and Peter was from the town of Bethsaida.

Philip found Nathanael and told him, "We have found the one Moses wrote about in the Law and about whom the prophets also wrote, Jesus of Nazareth, the son of Joseph."

"Nazareth! Can anything good come from there?" Nathanael asked.

"Come and see," said Philip. (1:44–46)

When people seem to say, "Can anything good come from Pindo, Lima, Chiclayo, or Reque?"

Roma Lee has simply followed Christ and said, "Come and see."

John Doty, MD
Austin, Texas

Adventures with Roma Lee: Sower of Seeds

"Sow your seed in the morning,
And at evening let your hands not be idle,
For you do not know which will succeed,
Whether this or that,
Or whether both will do equally well."
—Ecclesiastes 11:6

During the 1980s, several of my friends and I enjoyed high adventure trips. We had a regular schedule of float trips in the spring and backpacking trips in the fall. In the spring of 1989, no trip was planned, so when my brother, Jim, asked me to go on a medical mission trip to Peru, I said, "Sure." Little did I know how impactful that trip would be.

Roma Lee Courvisier was the group leader for the trip. The team first met each other in a quiet corner of the Miami airport. Roma Lee exuded joy and humor as she explained the details of the trip. She had a sparkle in her eye and a mischievous manner that made a mission trip seem like we were getting away with something. I'm sure others would agree that Roma Lee is the best stand-up comedian we have ever met. No matter the inevitable things that went wrong, Roma Lee maintained a calm manner. She strove to follow God's schedule, not her own.

Our first morning in Peru, Roma Lee led the team up a hill to the community of Caja de Aqua. It is named for the community's only source of water, a small concrete box with a water faucet that served the entire community. We visited with families in the community and returned later to attend church. On the hill, we could look over Lima, a city, at the time, of seven million. Smoggy air impaired our view and the task ahead loomed large.

While seeing people in nearby barrios, I examined emaciated children with rotted teeth and rusty hair. When children are extremely malnourished, they can no longer generate the pigment needed to turn their hair black. The children's growth was stunted and their arms and legs were like twigs. The plight of the children affected me the most, as my wife and I had children of the same age.

I saw untreated diseases causing significant disabilities. I saw houses made of thatch on hillsides barren due to the lack of rain. I saw whole communities that relied on water delivered by trucks to cisterns outside homes. In late January 1991, these truck and cisterns became the avenue of infection of the first cholera epidemic in Peru since 1867. By late December that year, over 320,000 Peruvians, mostly the desperately poor, had been infected and over 2,000 had died (paho.org).

I visited a woman named Vicki whose home was high up on one these hillsides. As we climbed the switchbacks to her home, we passed a new church under construction with mud bricks. Though Vicki had few resources, she closed her sewing business for five days so her neighbors could be seen by visiting doctors and nurses. On a brown paper wall separating the only two inside rooms, she had written, "'*Todo lo puedo en Cristo que me fortalice.' Filipenses 4:13.*" ("I can do all things through Christ who strengthens me." Philippians 4:13 [NIV].)

I was humbled by the tremendous gap between the sacrifice Vicki had made for the week and the one I had made. That week, she had, out of her poverty, put in everything—all she had to live on. I had given out of my surplus.

At the time, Roma Lee was leading ten to twelve teams to Peru, Ecuador, and Panama every year. When I found this out, I though she must be independently wealthy with a full-time team working for her. As it turned out, I was wrong. Roma Lee had simply learned to live by faith, believing that if God calls you, He is able to send you.

I came to understand that what powered Roma Lee was the gospel. In our country, some people try to defend the gospel as though it were weak. Truth is, the gospel is strong and needs to be lived. Roma Lee sets the standard for living the gospel. She is magnetic and as a result she draws people to Christ.

Many of us taking trips did so on a regular basis. Roma Lee called us "Repeat Offenders." These Repeat Offenders became Roma Lee's seeds. She has sown many of these Repeat Offenders throughout Latin America: Ken Biron, Paul Martorana, and Wanda and John Cox, in Peru; Jon and Karen Lambert, in Ecuador; Paul and Kattia Jones, in Bolivia; Bill and Shirley Beltz, in Nicaragua; Mitch Dooley, on the board of the Latin America

Children's Fund. As I confronted degrading, grinding poverty and suffering children, I was unable to just walk away. I decided that I also needed to be a Repeat Offender and joined additional brigades to Peru.

In April 1992, a trip to Peru was cancelled due to the civil war. Instead, our team went to Nicaragua in September and met Dr. Nour and Carolyn Sirker. Nour is a Nicaraguan surgeon who trained in the United States but chose to move to Nicaragua after a devastating earthquake that destroyed Managua in December 1972, killing five thousand people. After the Sandinistas took power in 1979, Nour and Carolyn went into exile in Florida. When democracy returned to Nicaragua in 1992 and the Sandinistas were voted out of power, they returned again to Nicaragua.

On the 1992 trip to Managua, a construction team began building a clinic that continues to operate today as Clinica Providencia. Dr. Sirker's mother donated land for the Escuela Christiana Emilia de Sirker in Barrio Santa Rosa. Mission teams built the school and continue to do maintenance. Fundacion el Samaritoano was funded to oversee the school. The Repeat Offenders Bill and Shirley Beltz started the Nicaraguan Christian Education Foundation child sponsorship program to raise funds for operating the school.

Does Escuela Sirker make a difference? Jose Aparicio Artola was thought to be learning disabled. His older sisters were accepted at Escuela Sirker, but Carolyn and Dofia Maritza, the school administrator, were reluctant to accept Jose, for the school had no provision for handicapped children. Once in a caring Christian environment, Jose thrived, became an excellent student, and is now a medical doctor. The success of Jose and other students would not have been possible except for mission teams led by Roma Lee working with Nour and Carolyn to further God's kingdom.

On two trips in the early 1990s, teams traveled to Bluefields on Nicaragua's Caribbean coast. We landed on a dirt runway with jungle on each side. The teams pitched tents in the basement of a Moravian church. We showered out of barrels of water. We were blessed to attend the Moravian church on Sunday. Although all the surfaces inside the church were hard, the congregation filled the church with hymns sung slowly in beautiful Caribbean Creole.

In addition to providing medical and dental care in Bluefields, the teams traveled to Laguna de Perias and Rama Cay in long, narrow dugout canoes powered by outboard engines. One day when traveling to Laguana de Perlas in three canoes, two of the canoes arrived together, but the third, with Roma Lee on board, was not to be seen. We waited and waited and waited some more. One of the two canoes went back to check for the third canoe. Eventually, after about one and one-half hours, the third canoe landed with a story that is emblematic of Roma Lee's character.

The cowling on the outboard motor powering her canoe had blown off. The cowling was very precious to the crew, so they began diving to recover it. Roma Lee noted a small collection of houses on the shore. Given that team members weren't going anywhere until the cowling was found, Roma Lee had the team climb up the embankment, set up a clinic, and provide care to the families. Rather than expressing frustration that matters were not going according to her plans, Roma Lee seized the opportunity to be a part of God's plan.

Roma Lee has experienced health issues, particularly lupus, which limited the countries in which she could work. Time and time again, Roma Lee has chosen to lead trips when others might use an excuse of poor health to justify reducing their commitment. Volunteer is what one does on one's own time. Sacrifice is what one does on someone else's time. Roma Lee has sacrificed her plans and answered God's call multiple times.

Over the years, Roma Lee has ministered to many people in many countries. She has planted many seeds. Her hands have not been idle, nurturing seeds to further the gospel. She has mentored and challenged many who have made trips with her and others who have only known her in North America. Now, Roma Lee has reached the point at which leading future trips is not possible. She has run with perseverance the race marked out for her. Now it is the time for us who have been mentored by Roma Lee, her seeds, to carry on her work.

Top: Roma Lee with Paul Jones, missionary to Bolivia.
Bottom: Son-in-law, Steve Grout, examining eyes of children in Peru.

Top: Roma Lee with Jon and Karen Lambert, missionaries to Ecuador.
Bottom: Daughter Elaine in Peru.

Top: Roma Lee with daughter, Lynette at school for the deaf in Peru.
Bottom: Daughter Lee Ann in Nicaragua.

CHAPTER 13

A Life Well Lived

Roma Lee's newsletter sharing her retirement decision:

December 2011

Rejoice, A Savior Has Come!

"Thou are worthy, O Lord, to receive glory and honor..."
Revelation 4:11a. (KJV)

To all who have shared in my life, you have helped to make these eighty-three years a wonderful journey—and I'm not home yet!

This year completes sixty-two years in full-time ministry. I have spent thirty-one years as a pastor's wife and have now spent thirty-one years serving in missions. There have been hundreds of you right beside me. You are the great and the strong in leadership. You have challenged and inspired me. You have never ceased to love, to give, to go, and to pray. There are not enough words to express the depth of my gratitude to the Lord and to you.

I have had serious health problems for several years. Arriving back from my last trip to South America, I was taken directly to the hospital from the airport.

My problems are not new. I was in the hospital a few years ago with congestive heart failure, kidney failure, and lung infection. These problems have become much worse. I have had lupus for 20+ years. I hope you will understand why I am no longer able to travel overseas. I will forever love and miss the precious people in many countries. I will greatly miss all of you who have been part of my life. I would love to keep in touch with you. It would be an honor to be a prayer partner with you. What joy it would be to receive news of you and your family and to receive pictures, too!

A big thanks to you and praise to the Lord for answered prayers. There are now enough funds to feed the children and staff at R.L.C. (Roma Lee Courvisier) School for more than three years with money to cover some growth and inflation. They receive two meals a day—breakfast and lunch.

At this wonderful season of the year, may God give you special and abundant blessings.

Keep telling the story of Jesus and His love.

Edward Everett Hale said, "I am only one, but I am one. I cannot do everything, but I can do something. And because I cannot do everything, I will not refuse to do the something that I can do. What I can do, I should do. And what I should do, by the grace of God, I will do."

With love, joy and a grateful heart,
Roma Lee

Roma Lee shared her gratefulness for the support of her family through her years of ministry.

"Our family has always been a ministry team. All three daughters – Elaine, Lee Ann and Lynette have gone with me to mission fields. They have each been to several countries.

I recall one particular trip, I was in Bogota, Colombia, with Mendosa Taylor at the same time that Lynette was in the jungles of Colombia on a mission trip. I would look out the window of the small plane at the jungles below and wonder where my child was. Lynette would say we never felt closer than when we were the furthest apart. I wrote a personal message on each page of the devotional *Our Daily Bread*. Lynette would never read a day ahead because she knew she would get a message from her mom each day.

It has been a blessing beyond words to see the love for God's work in the lives of my children and to experience mission trips with them. They have always encouraged and supported me in all I have tried to do. Their love and care has been strong during the 25 years of Frank's illness. Lynette and Steve have always been near to make visits, take frosties and take care of any need when I was away.

I have lived with Lynette, Steve, Jeannette and Jackson for many years. Thank you Lynette for all the trips to and from the airport and for the thousand and one things you do for me to make my life comfortable and good. Thanks Steve for adopting me and always helping with my needs. It would have been easier to adopt a child to raise. Yet, you are always helping and never complaining. Jeannette and Jackson probably thought I just came with the other household things. They have been helpful and always made life fun. Now they are a strong arm to lean on. Thanks kids!

It has been a wonderful experience to have all my grandchildren go on mission trips with me. Some have gone several times. Sharing the joy with me were: Christopher and his wife Tiffanie; Lori and her husband Chris; Zac, Kayla, Jeannette and Jackson.

I have written 3rd John 1:4 in the front of all my Bibles, "I have no greater joy than to hear that my children (and grandchildren and great grandchildren) are walking in the truth." God bless you all.

I have one sibling, my brother Lynn. He has gone with me to Ecuador and Peru; his wife, Brenda to Peru and Ecuador. Their son, Scott went with me to Costa Rica and Panama.

Thank you family!"

As Roma Lee recalled her ministry, she spoke these words; "God will use any of us if we let Him. I always knew there was one person that I had to follow up with. It was Patricia in Guatemala, the old man in Peru with the dying daughter who needed medicine, the child named Janete in Nicaragua. I always knew there was someone, somewhere who needed my help. If God calls you, He will enable you to do what He wants. In Ecuador, from the first time of having the dream of the people starving in Meridiano, I simply got up the next day knowing that I had to get an airline ticket and raise money. I made calls, contacted people, and raised $12,000 for the first trip to feed the starving people. On my last trip, we were able to take $85,470 to feed the hungry people of Ecuador. I wouldn't have known what to do if God hadn't told me."

She continued, "I believe that life experiences helped to prepare me for God's call. My heart was moved by the needs of His people who were starving. I have had just enough poverty, disappointment, and pain to feel the hurt of others. I knew I must do something to help the suffering in Ecuador. All of Ecuador was in need of help. They were hungry. The desperate need would continue for many years."

The question most asked of me was, "How did you raise the funds?"

"I believe people have tender hearts if you tell the story of need. We can speak for those who cannot speak for themselves. When people give to meet those needs, you have to stay connected with them. People want to know the difference their giving has made. For me, it was simply staying connected with people, continuing to tell the story, and sharing the victories. Above all, each effort must be covered with prayer. Whatever plan works for you, just do it."

After a lifetime of service to Christ, Roma Lee still has a firm commitment to the spread of the gospel.

She stated, "I still have the same passion in my heart; my body just wore out. I never felt afraid in a foreign country. I never felt afraid in the jungles at night. I loved the people that I first saw dying of starvation in Mexico. My heart was moved, and I decided that if I could do anything to help them, I would do it. The door to missions is to work wherever you are. There are people to work with everywhere, but there is less help overseas. I fell in love with people everywhere I went. It was a joy, not a sacrifice, to go wherever the Lord wanted me to go. Wherever there is something you can do for people in the Name of the Lord, do it. The center of God's will is where I want to be."

She also shared these words, "I have put every ounce of me into everything. I have never been weary in spirit. The Lord gave me physical strength enough to do the work, even with lupus.

Until the last day, I never grew weary of the Lord's work. I had the same passion on the last trip as I did for the first one. Don't faint in the work He has called you to do. The Lord will renew spiritual strength even when physical strength is gone. I love to hear the roar of jungle planes; I felt that I did mount up with wings of eagles. I am reminded of God's power to take us places we never dreamed of going."

She continued, "The people are just as precious here at home as in other countries. God can give you a deep-seated joy and peace, even in the hard times. He brings all of the blessings. When you get far enough down the line and look back, you will see the blessings and the people He has brought into your life."

One of Roma Lee's favorite scriptures has truly sustained her life at all levels throughout her ministry. "But they that wait upon the Lord, shall renew their strength; they shall mount up with wings as eagles; they shall run, and not be weary; and they shall walk, and not faint" (Isaiah 40:31 KJV).

About the Author

Dr. Bonnie Newell graduated from Anderson University with a Bachelor of Arts in elementary education; from Anderson School of Theology with a Master of Religious Education; and from Trinity Theological Seminary with a Doctor of Religious Studies. Dr. Newell has worked with children for over thirty-five years as a teacher, children's pastor, and mentor. She has been on mission trips to Panama, Japan, Hong Kong, Ecuador, Peru, Nicaragua, Kenya, and Haiti. She is the author of the children's book *Oh, My Goodness.*

Made in the USA
Charleston, SC
24 February 2014